What people are saying about

Mescalito Riding His White Horse

The visionary music of bluegrass songster Peter Rowan captured Mike Fiorito's attention leading him on a deep spiritual trek. Rowan tells of his mentors from Bill Monroe to Harry Smith, Buddha and beyond. *Mescalito* is Fiorito's gripping narrative of his journey into a new musical consciousness.
Dr. Neil Rosenberg, Professor Emeritus, Department of Folklore at Memorial University of Newfoundland, St. John's, NL, and author of *Bluegrass Generation*

Wow! [*Mescalito*] is beautiful. I'm touched that you "got" it!
Peter Rowan

This wide-ranging book is obviously a labor of love: love of music and love of and admiration for Peter Rowan. Along the way the reader is showered with anecdotes from the author's interviews and introduced to the soul lurking in the depths of Rowan's compositions and varied delivery styles. Who would have guessed Asian spiritual philosophy and wisdom to be found in Bluegrass music and its derivatives? For anyone interested in gaining an in-depth acquaintance and knowledge of legendary musician Peter Rowan and the music he composed and performed, this book cannot be recommended highly enough.
Dr. Art Funkhouser, Jungian psychotherapist (https://arthur. funkhouser.ch/en/)

In *Mescalito Riding His White Horse*, Mike Fiorito creates one of the greatest music interviews ever. His poetic prose and personal anecdotes bring a wonderful sparkle to Peter Rowan's musical and spiritual odyssey. From Buddhism to the intelligence of birds, and from psychedelic rock to the history of bluegrass, this short book is an inspiring meditation on music, life, and everything in between. But most importantly, what makes this book special is, in essence, what Mike so eloquently describes it to be, an attempt to discover "the source of what it is to be human."

Anthony Peake, author of *The Hidden Universe* (https://www.anthonypeake.com/)

You did a great job with the book! Really got to the heart of Peter's vibe.

Christopher Henry, member of the Peter Rowan Bluegrass Band (https://www.noyamountainmusic.com/about-chris-henry/)

Other Titles by this Author

The Hated Ones
ISBN: 978-1599541747

Sleeping with Fishes
ISBN: 978-1948651264

Falling from Trees
ISBN: 978-1627203333

Call Me Guido
ISBN: 978-1733994804

Hallucinating Huxley
ISBN: 978-1790385768

Freud's Haberdashery Habit: & other stories
ISBN: 978-1723540936

Mescalito Riding His White Horse

Inspired by The Musical Adventures
of Peter Rowan

Mescalito Riding His White Horse[1]

Inspired by The Musical Adventures
of Peter Rowan

Mike Fiorito

BOOKS

Winchester, UK
Washington, USA

JOHN HUNT PUBLISHING

First published by O-Books, 2024
O-Books is an imprint of John Hunt Publishing Ltd., 3 East St., Alresford,
Hampshire SO24 9EE, UK
office@jhpbooks.com
www.johnhuntpublishing.com
www.o-books.com

For distributor details and how to order please visit the 'Ordering' section on our website.

ISBN: 978 1 80341 118 7
978 1 80341 119 4 (ebook)
Library of Congress Control Number: 2022934836

A CIP catalogue record for this book is available from the British Library.

Design: Lapiz Digital Services

UK: Printed and bound by CPI Group (UK) Ltd, Croydon, CR0 4YY
Printed in North America by CPI GPS partners

We operate a distinctive and ethical publishing philosophy in
all areas of our business, from our global network of authors to
production and worldwide distribution.

Contents

Acknowledgements

I am indebted to the many people who contributed to *Mescalito Riding His White Horse*. The experience of creating this book has led me on a journey of research and discovery from which I have not yet returned. I feel immensely privileged and thankful to have been inspired by Peter Rowan's music and mystical vision.

The idea for *Mescalito* came to me in a flash, after a few conversations with Peter, along with many close listenings of his music. When I told my wife, Arielle, that I wanted to write about how bluegrass gave birth to the universe, or something like that, she understandably looked at me a little sideways. Before I knew what I wanted to write I had only a sketch of the project in my head. I knew that it would be very unconventional: a mixture of interview, visions, and memoir.

I am grateful to the many reviews and inputs that I received from Arielle, Susan Kaessinger, Angela Welch, Bill Bernthal, and Nancy Graham. We worked like a well-oiled team.

I am likewise indebted to Christopher Henry, Myron Dyal, Anthony Peake, Frank Serio and Art Funkhouser for their readings, support, and insights. Thank you to bluegrass scholar Neil Rosenberg for his corrections on some of the details related to bluegrass history.

Thank you also to Yungchen Lhamo for introducing me to Peter and to Juan Carlos Pinto for making the portrait of Ernie Paniccioli, which inspired the origin of *Mescalito*. We were fated to meet in this lifetime.

And finally, a huge bow of gratitude to Peter Rowan for his belief in the project. Not really knowing who I was initially, Peter spent a great deal of time with me on the phone, corresponding via text and e-mail, and made time to meet me near his home in California. Peter was patient, kind and good humored during our back and forth. I was deeply honored to have earned Peter's trust in the process. As I told Peter, listening to his stories, and getting to know him, on some level, was enough.

It's like déjà vu all over again.
—Yogi Berra

When iron birds fly in the sky and when the horse moves across the land, the Buddha will be in the land of the Redface.
—Padmasambhava

Time is the substance from which I am made. Time is a river which carries me along, but I am the river; it is a tiger that devours me, but I am the tiger; it is a fire that consumes me, but I am the fire.
—Jorge Luis Borges

From the time without beginning
All my ancient parents
Have shown me great kindness
In lifetime after lifetime,
In confusion and sorrow
We wander now in darkness
Birth old age sickness death
Like a shadow close behind.

When I think of how you loved me
And you care for me so kindly
Fed and clothed me and kept me from all harm
Oh, I want to take you with me
Across Samsara's waters
Like a child running to its mother's arms

Love and compassion
Lightning flashing
Oh sufferers do cry

Let every living, breathing being
Find happiness.
Let wisdom mind
Bodhicitta mind.
Arise!
—"Arise" (*Dharma Blues*, Peter Rowan)

Reality is imagined.
—Mike Fiorito

Foreword

by Peter Rowan

Although I have led a sometimes-troubled life with no special gift of genius, Mike Fiorito has allowed some of my spiritual journey in music to appear as an inspiration for him to tell his own story. My mind harkens to our forebears who showed a light on mankind's journey from darkness. This is our lineage of inspired humanity. From African griots chanting the genealogies, to the Greek poets singing their epic tales, to the chanted lineages of enlightened masters in the vast Himalayas, the blues, bluegrass, and rock and roll here at home, all cultures of our world share the great oral traditions carried like a sacred flame from one encampment to another, sharing. If we look deeply enough, this inspiration is available to all, to enrich our lives and to benefit others. Mike Fiorito's insight into the interconnectedness of all phenomenal appearances is an invitation to appreciate how intertwined our humanity is, the subtle manifestations of our aspirations as dwellers on this planet. As Bill Monroe said to me one day on that endless highway, somewhere in Scotland, "Don't ever give up, Pete, don't ever give up!" It is my hope the reader will enjoy this journey!

The more enlightened our houses are, the more their walls ooze ghosts.
—Italo Calvino

I Have Sung Illusion's Songs[2]

This book was inspired by several interviews conducted with Peter Rowan over a period of a few months during 2021. When I interviewed Peter for *Atwood Magazine*, it became clear to me that a conventional article wouldn't adequately express what I had come to learn about him. I wrote the article anyway but began thinking about a larger project. Not only a musician and songwriter, Peter is also a poet, magus, mystic, and mentor. In addition to possessing a trove of bluegrass history and lore, I discovered that Peter has extensive knowledge of psychedelics, Buddhism, and other wisdom traditions. And, most importantly, Peter lives the teachings he's learned.

Prior to the cultural upheavals of the 1960s, Peter spent several years in Nashville absorbing its folklore and musical traditions after touring with Bill Monroe & His Bluegrass Boys. Learning from people as diverse in their worldviews as Bill Monroe and Jerry Garcia gave Peter insight into the crosscurrents of America. Its connective tissue. The upside-down and inside-out riptides. The frayed patterns on the inside of the quilt—as well as the magnificent designs on the outside, meant to be seen.

All that said, this is not a biography.

During the time I wrote this book I listened repeatedly to Peter's entire catalog. So much so that my ten-year-old son, Travis, was often heard singing (in a high lonesome bluegrass voice), "The free Mexican air force/Mescalito riding his white horse,"[3] to make fun of his father. But at least I knew he was listening. To nourish my writing, I shamelessly plundered several Buddhist, Hindu, American Indigenous, and Western esoteric texts. I felt that in order to properly represent his music, I had to reflect the many cultures and voices that Peter draws from to create his music. Of course, I've also quoted or referenced Peter's song lyrics with permission from his publisher, sometimes embedding them into the prose. For clarity, all quoted lyrics are end-noted. As I said to Peter, we innovated a new prose form to make this book happen.

I wrote this book because from the moment I first spoke with Peter in early 2021 to the present, I have voyaged to the origins of music. This journey shattered my previously held notions of chronological time. As I explored deeper, it occurred to me that music can skate the surface of an emotion or thought or it can take you to the center of the cosmos. In our everyday lives we listen to music to make us happy, to make us dance, to make us sing. Music can connect us to a deeper spirituality. Consider the choral music of Bach and Palestrina or Tibetan chanting. In the Amazon, shamans sing songs, or icaros, that produce powerful visions in the listener.

Peter's music has tapped into this transformational potential. He never pursued the path of rock superstar—Peter was more interested in the alchemical process of music. In discovering this magic for myself, I have been projected across time, place, and identity and tried to put that experience into words. I have discovered that what makes Peter's music special is the authenticity of his message. There is also a rare vulnerability in Peter's music that comes from his spiritual centeredness. For a person with his life experience, having played with the great Bill Monroe and many other music icons, Peter is very down to earth. I hear the man in his music. Not just the public performance of a persona.

Except for the quoted interviews, which were transcribed as spoken, what follows is a combination of autobiography mixed with my visions and dreams. Some were imagined. All were real.

The Musical Adventures of Peter Rowan

I've been a fan of Peter Rowan since listening to the *Old & In the Way* album when I was in my teens in the 1970s. As a kid from Queens, I didn't grow up listening to bluegrass and country. *Old & In the Way* exposed my generation, especially those of us who lived in cities, to the bluegrass music of Bill Monroe, the Stanley Brothers, Flatt & Scruggs, Roy Acuff, and others. *Old & In the Way* is so explosive, so full of ravishing beauty and energy, that it appeared to come screaming out of the sky on a chariot of fire. Featuring Jerry Garcia on banjo, Vassar Clements on fiddle, and David Grisman on mandolin, *Old & In the Way* blasted open a portal to another universe. Listening to that album launched me on a personal spiritual and musical journey to which I see no end.

Listening to *Old & In the Way* makes me happy. I can't resist tapping my foot to the quicksilver speed of the instrumentals and singing along with the angelic harmonies. Like all American music, bluegrass is a composite of the many cultures that came together on American soil. Bluegrass reaches far back beyond Bill Monroe into what Greil Marcus called that "weird old America, a playground of God, Satan, tricksters, Puritans, confidence men, illuminati, braggarts, preachers, anonymous poets of all stripes."

But Bill Monroe codified bluegrass as a unique musical form. According to Thomas Goldsmith, "Monroe wanted to give back to farm and country people his imaginative reworking of the sounds he heard while growing up in Rosine, Kentucky. He was recreating a fabled childhood that included moonlight rides with his Uncle Pen, bereft days after both parents had died and his brothers went away, and fiddle tunes that literally echoed 'high on a hill and above the town.'" There's a gallop pace in bluegrass unlike any other form of American music. As Bill

Monroe told Peter Rowan, to play bluegrass you must "follow the horse's hooves."

Bluegrass incorporated elements of old-time, blues, country, ragtime, and even Hawaiian music. As Peter Rowan said, Bill talked about his "other" music, the mellifluous Hawaiian sound, like speaking of a secret lover. But bluegrass was faster and harder. If you unspool the coils of bluegrass, you'll discover the roots of all American music. In fact, you can draw a line from Monroe to the Louvin Brothers, to the Everly Brothers, to the Beatles. The building blocks of bluegrass are cloaked in its speed and ferocity. Like Bill Monroe said, "I would have made a fine bluesman if I hadn't invented bluegrass."

Bill Monroe knew that rhythm, drive, and harmonies make people dance and sing. People would shout out at Bill Monroe's live concerts, hooting and hollering. There is a raging fire in bluegrass, a resistance, a break with everything that preceded it. Bluegrass, at its best, is an expression of joy, of lust and transcendence. In his book, *Earl Scruggs and the Foggy Mountain Breakdown*, Thomas Goldsmith wrote that Monroe introduced higher-pitched harmonies than were used in old-time music. The higher-pitched harmonies in bluegrass have an ethereal quality. Calling your soul, like a million saints in heaven, to paradise. To ecstasy. Like angels sweetly whispering in your ear.

In an interview with Terry Gross on NPR, Peter said, "the harmonies on 'God's Own Child' are a really old-school style of gospel singing. It's a style I learned from Bill Monroe, who called it holiness singing, and it was a style taught by itinerant preachers and choir instructors who came up through Kentucky and the Carolinas and Virginia, oh, back before the turn of the twentieth century."

If Bill Monroe is considered the father of bluegrass, Peter Rowan is its international ambassador. No one since Bill Monroe has written more original bluegrass songs than Rowan.

And although there is a through line of bluegrass spanning the six decades of his career, Rowan has continued to reinvent himself. He's composed and recorded reggae, rock, Hawaiian, Buddhist, Tex-Mex, psychedelic, and country music. And he's collaborated and performed with the best musicians of our time, including Clarence White, Buell Neidlinger, Ricky Skaggs, Alison Krauss, Gillian Welch, Yungchen Lhamo, Mike Auldridge, David Grisman, Jerry Garcia, Tony Rice, Flaco Jiménez, Vassar Clements, and many others. Rowan's extensive discography reflects the incredible breadth of his career.

A Grammy Award winner and six-time nominee, Rowan plays guitar and mandolin, yodels, and sings. He has written too many great songs to mention them all. Some of my favorites are "Vulture Peak," "While the Ocean Roars," "On the Blue Horizon," "Midnight Moonlight," "Medicine Trail," "Sweet Melinda," "Midnight Highway," "The Light in Carter Stanley's Eyes," and "Panama Red."

Rowan's catalog of albums is also impressive. Some of my favorite Rowan albums are *Medicine Trail*, *All on a Rising Day*, *The First Whippoorwill*, *Texican Badman*, *Yonder* (with Jerry Douglas), *You Were There for Me* (with Tony Rice), *Dharma Blues*, *Legacy*, and *Carter Stanley's Eyes*.

Born in Wayland, Massachusetts to a musical family, Rowan learned to play guitar from his uncle. He spent his teenage years absorbing the sights and sounds of the Hillbilly Ranch, a legendary country music nightclub in Boston frequented by acts like the Lilly Brothers and Tex Logan. In 1956 Peter Rowan formed his first band, the Cupids, while still in high school.

I spoke with Peter for the first time in April 2021.

Let me give a little backstory. A few weeks prior, I had interviewed Yungchen Lhamo, the international Tibetan singer who had performed and recorded with Rowan. Yuncheng is incredibly adaptable. Her magical voice is sometimes delicately woven around African kora, Middle Eastern percussion, steel guitar, flamenco guitar, strings, or piano.

When I asked Yungchen how she'd met Rowan, she asked if I would like to talk to him. Trying not to sound too eager, I meekly said yes. A few minutes later Yungchen texted me Rowan's mobile number.

He's waiting for you to call.

I admit I was a little nervous. I'd long been a fan of bluegrass, but while I am knowledgeable of the genre, I wouldn't say I'm an expert. I learned a lot about bluegrass from my friend Greg Grady, who turned me on to his vast record collection in the nineties. I went to jazz, folk, and bluegrass music shows with Greg when he lived in New York City. His wall-to-wall collection was something to behold, as was his vast knowledge of who played with whom, when, on what label, and so on.

Rowan and I spoke the next night. It was magical to listen to the voice I'd heard singing in my head for nearly forty years speaking softly over the phone line. Rowan was easy to talk to, funny and very smart.

"How did a kid from Wayland, Massachusetts, get an audition with Bill Monroe?" I asked.

"There was a big bluegrass scene in Harvard Square starting in the fifties. And there were also pickers in the country, just outside the city. In about 1962, I met Joe Val [real name Valiante], who was passionate about bluegrass. Val was the link between college kids and bluegrass lovers. Val had met Tex Logan when Logan was a student at MIT. Logan was kind of a technical genius, but he also loved bluegrass and country music. Logan and Val played at the Hillbilly Ranch, a legendary country music nightclub in Boston. I spent my teenage years absorbing the sights and sounds of this scene."

Tex Logan could not pronounce Valiante's Italian last name, thus introducing Joe onstage as Joe "Val." Rowan was about sixteen at the time; Val and Logan were some fifteen years older. Though Rowan also played with his rock band, the Cupids, he turned more of his attention to bluegrass.

"Tell me about Val."

"Val was down to earth. He was a typewriter repairman. Val searched out the essence of bluegrass. In doing so, he became an emanation of Bill Monroe in mandolin and vocal style. Of course, he gave it his own lifeblood. In this circle of players was Bill Keith, who had played banjo with Monroe as a Bluegrass Boy on the Grand Ole Opry. Keith lived in the Boston area and often got together with Jim Rooney—guitarist, singer, and music producer. Jim Rooney was studying ancient epic ballad traditions at Harvard as well as singing bluegrass with his musical partner Bill Keith, who was reinventing the five-string banjo bluegrass style."

According to Rowan, the corridor of bluegrass music went from Boston to Pennsylvania, down Highway 81 (formerly Route 17) to West Virginia and the Shenandoah Valley. From there the circuit continued into Kentucky and Tennessee. For some reason, it skipped the thriving New York City folk scene. Val went on to play with the Charles River Valley Boys, a group formed in Cambridge, Massachusetts. At the time, Keith and Rooney needed a mandolin player. Since Rowan had been playing around the scene, Val eventually asked him to take his place with Keith and Rooney, and they toured for a while as Keith, Rooney and Rowan.

With the folk revival in full swing, groups like Flatt & Scruggs immediately recognized the potential for a lucrative new audience in cities and on college campuses in the North, but Monroe was slower to respond. Under the influence of Ralph Rinzler, a young musician and folklorist from New Jersey who briefly became Monroe's manager in 1963, Monroe gradually expanded his geographic reach beyond the traditional Southern country music circuit. Rinzler wrote a lengthy profile of Monroe in the influential folk music magazine *Sing Out!* that for the first time publicly referred to Monroe as the "Father of Bluegrass."

Intending to bring visibility to Monroe, Rinzler put a band together for him that included Keith. As Rowan had played with Keith, Rowan was hired to sing lead and play guitar, performing next to the burning fire of Bill Monroe. As is common in bluegrass, singers often projected their harmonies directly at each other. But Bill Monroe wanted his singers to lean in, shoulder to shoulder, to make sure the voices became one, as if transmuted in a volcanic blaze.

"We did a long weekend of gigs all over New England. During this time, Monroe asked Keith to help me. Keith then invited me to what they called back then the 'DJ convention' in Nashville. The event was just for musicians and DJs. There weren't any fans there. The convention was very eye-opening for me. I met icons as they sat around and played. And I learned that, despite the formulaic Nashville style, there were a lot of jazz musicians in Nashville. With jazz and big bands on the decline, musicians switched over to bluegrass and country. There were countless studio musicians in Nashville like Hank 'Sugarfoot' Garland, Junior Huskey, and guitarist Chet Atkins who were schooled in jazz. Keep in mind, people like Patsy Cline and Jim Reeves were jazz-influenced singers."

"Why did you leave Bill Monroe?"

"You have to remember I was about twenty-two. Monroe was about fifty-five at the time. I could have just stayed and played with Monroe. But first, Monroe had problems paying sometimes. And—this was more important—I had to feel the fire in my own engine. I was bursting with songs and ideas. Let me also add that Monroe was grooming his son, James, to be the lead singer. I didn't want to stand in the wings. I wanted to find my own voice. The last show we did was at Whitey's Lounge in

Baltimore, which was also the first place we'd played together. Richard Greene on fiddle, James Monroe on bass. People said the music was so elevated, it felt like Monroe was giving me a sendoff in a rocket. Monroe had his own arc, his own agenda. But he understood me."

"What was one of the most important things you learned from Monroe?"

"Everyone played to the time of Monroe's impeccable mandolin and stark tenor voice," said Rowan. "Also, Bill taught me that music is very physical, all the way from trance dancing to crowding the microphone to sing a bluegrass duet. And Bill taught me to go for what he called 'the ancient tones.'"

After leaving Monroe, Rowan teamed up with David Grisman to form Earth Opera, a psychedelic group that frequently opened for the Doors.

"What was it like leaving Monroe to play in Earth Opera? You wrote all the songs. It was like, as you said, you had socked away a whole bunch of ideas and had them at the ready."

"I wrote all of the songs in Nashville. Then I showed them to Porter Wagoner. Wagoner had taken a liking to me. One time, between shows at the Opry, Bashful Brother Oswald, Roy Acuff's dobro player, took me down to Roy's new museum on Broadway. They showed me big jars of moonshine that fans had brought in for them. Roy told me you know when the moonshine is good because it bubbles up a certain way. They call it frog's eyes. Then you know it's good to drink. Roy and Oswald insisted I drink some of the moonshine. Oswald said, 'Have ye some, Pete, heh, heh, Bill won't mind!'

"I replied, 'No thanks, Bill, he's got eyes in the back of his mind!' They were trying to see how green I really was!"

When he played the Earth Opera songs for Wagoner, Wagoner said that the songs weren't for a country audience; they were for listeners of Rowan's generation.

Rowan went on to make many records with various groups.

"I was always a seeker of different kinds of music. I wasn't content to keep doing the same thing repeatedly. David Grisman put on a record for me of Ry Cooder playing with Flaco Jiménez, a Tex-Mex (Tejano) accordion player. I loved that sound. I then went to Texas to meet and play with Jiménez. He was already renowned. He had me come out to a gig out in the Texas Hill Country at a place called Irene and Fidel's. The venue had chicken wire windows; it was an outdoor/indoor dance hall."

The result of these sessions was his first solo album, entitled *Peter Rowan* (1978). It showcased a mix of country, Tex-Mex, rock, and bluegrass. Featuring Richard Greene (fiddle), Flaco Jiménez (accordion), Tex Logan (fiddle, violin), and Buell Neidlinger (bass), the album has iconic versions of "Free Mexican Airforce," "Midnight Moonlight," and "Land of the Navajo" and a breakout live performance of "Panama Red." Half of the album was recorded in Texas and the other half at McCabe's Guitar Shop in Los Angeles.

Over the years, Rowan's musical adventures continued to lead him to explore other genres. A self-professed Buddhist, Rowan recorded *Dharma Blues* in 2014, showing just how far he can stretch. The songs on *Dharma Blues* are bluegrass based but have rock, blues, jazz, and world music elements. The songs reach back to some faraway place in American history. "Restless Grave" has echoes of the old American West. I can hear winds whip across the Dust Bowl. I see tumbleweed rolling through an old bootleg town. Featuring other thoughtfully written tunes like "River of Time," "Wisdom Woman," "Raven," and "My Love Will Never Change," *Dharma Blues* includes guest appearances from Jack Casady (Jefferson Airplane, Hot Tuna) and vocalist Gillian Welch, with instrumentation ranging from banjo and pedal steel to harmonium and water drum. I've seen a YouTube video of Rowan performing "Arise" solo between shows. In this on-the-spot live version, there are no dials or mixing boards to fix anything. And nothing needs fixing. He sings "Arise" beautifully, hitting the high notes with ease, plucking his guitar in an open tuning. In this setting the lyrics come across clearly. That performance alone is telling of Rowan's mastery.

In another interview, Peter said, "Tibetan music shares a similarity with bluegrass. They're both from remote mountainous areas populated by hill country people. Like Tibetan music, bluegrass has a very rootsy sound, earthy, and yet with spiritual overtones, both in the straight and the sacred songs. They have a kind of longing, a yearning for transcendence."

I asked him about his performances with Yungchen Lhamo.

"Yungchen blew everyone away. She has no barrier to the audience. When we'd go into an instrumental, she'd amble out into the audience and get everybody dancing. It was magical. Imagine a relatively tame Florida audience that came to hear bluegrass. Suddenly this beautiful Tibetan dakini comes out to them in their seats and leads them by the hand into ecstatic dancing."

Yungchen and Rowan did several radio shows and outdoor festivals together. The song "I'm Calling You (From My Mountain)" features the dynamics of how their voices work together.

"She was brave. And incredibly compassionate. When we were on tour, Yungchen would go shopping for groceries and give them all away. While we were playing honky-tonks in Georgia, she'd minister to people. 'You must stop drinking.' She'd do things like take a cab or a bus to the airport seventy miles away. She didn't drive a car. But she was incredibly dedicated. This was tough on her. I don't think chasing the dragon of music around the world is Yungchen's thing. As for me, the road has been a dangerous addiction. All I've known. Constantly exploiting my gifts to justify my existence."

"What are you working on now?"

"I'm playing with Los Texmaniacs; they are protégés of Jiménez. We are called the Free Mexican Airforce."

The Free Mexican Airforce performs some of Rowan's most beloved songs: "Come Back to Old Santa Fe," "Ride the Wild Mustang," "Midnight Moonlight," and "Free Mexican Airforce."

Max Baca, a legend on the bajo sexto, a twelve-string guitar-like instrument, is in the group, along with his nephew Josh Baca, who is fast attaining legendary status on the accordion.

"I met Baca when he came onstage with Flaco and me at the Line Camp in Tesuque, New Mexico. He was twelve at the time. It's like I've come full circle. We expect to go on tour in the fall [of] 2021."

In addition to playing and touring with the Free Mexican Airforce, Rowan plays with other configurations such as Peter Rowan's Big Twang Theory, Peter Rowan's Twang an' Groove and Peter Rowan & Crucial Reggae.

"We've completed a collection of new material for Rebel, including a new version of 'From My Mountain' with Molly Tuttle, and Billy Strings jumped in and played guitar on two cuts!"

We can only expect to continue to be surprised by Peter Rowan. As I write this I hear Bill Monroe's advice, "Don't ever give up, Pete, don't ever give up!"

I was a rock on a snow-capped mountain
Falling snow, all I could see
A raindrop fell, a tear from heaven
Diamond ice imprisoned me

Om mane padme hum hri
Om mane padme hum hri

Sunlight shone down, the ice was melted
A tiny stream began to flow
Rolling me over and over and over down the mountain
In the crystal waters I did go

Om mane padme hum hri
Om mane padme hum hri

The rushing stream became a roaring river
Washed me clean to the edge of land
The moonlit waves, the indigo oceans
I am just a tiny grain of sand

Om mane padme hum hri
Om mane padme hum hri
— "A Grain of Sand" (*Dharma Blues*, Peter Rowan)

Sailing on the River of Time[4]

When I see old pictures of Peter playing with legends like Bill Monroe, Clarence White, and Jerry Garcia, I get sentimental, even emotional. But why should I? They are not my memories. They are Peter's. But I now relate to them as if they are mine too. When you research someone's sixty-year history, obsessively watch YouTube videos of their performances, look through old photos, listen to everything you can in their catalog, you begin to form a relationship with that person. You begin to talk to them when they're not there. You dream about them. You worry about them. I imagine how heavy it must be for Peter to look back on his storied career, having written classic tunes like "Panama Red" and "Land of the Navajo" and playing with some of the most influential musicians and songwriters of the day, many of whom have died. It's not just that the people have died. And it's not just about the music. The world of new hope and change that Peter's generation helped usher in seems to be fading in the rearview mirror.

In a video from 1965, Peter's chin is thin and narrow. He's about twenty-three years old, leaning into the microphone, singing across from Bill Monroe—younger than my son Thelonious is now. In the 1973 Warner Brothers television appearance of his band Muleskinner, Peter is tall and youthful but longhaired. You can see the rainbow shimmer of Panama Red emanating from his face. The players in Muleskinner have a psychedelic gleam, some wearing brightly colored clothes and long hippie hair.

My heart aches as I imagine the weight Peter carries in his soul of all those years and experiences as they recede into the background. How it must feel to have been a force that created the culture changes in the sixties. To have remembrances of a friendship with Bill Monroe that only a handful of people on

17

this planet could relate to. To have lost the great Clarence White in a tragic car accident, cut down way too early in his career. To have been a close friend of Jerry Garcia, now gone, who admired and encouraged Peter's songwriting.

I think of Peter as a friend, and our relationship as having grown organically. My friendship with Peter is different from my other friendships as Peter has stood shoulder to shoulder with giants. I feel like I am learning when I talk to Peter. I'm curious to hear his stories. He is a tale teller. He's funny. And he's very charming. As he once wrote to me in a text: *I lived in Texas, I know how to tell tall tales, lies, ballads, and fakery. I'll sell you some snake oil rejuvenated in a green glass bottle made by Mexican brujas on the waning moon of August!*

Jokes aside, Peter has remained humble and kind as long as I've known him. But it could be that I see him as more of a friend than he sees me. How could I ask him about that?

In one conversation I asked Peter, "What drives you to write and play music?"

"I saw how my parents suffered and how their world seemed determined by forces of business and obligations to social norms that made them unhappy. And I was born into a world at war, so I saw that music was one of the things that made people happy, and I devoted myself to becoming a conduit for music, to be useful somehow. And that has led me on my path. Outwardly I am an entertainer, shining a light, inwardly, well, the story goes on!"

Vision of the Dalai Lama

Before I began writing this book, I had a vision that I was visited by the Dalai Lama. Unlike the Dalai Lama I'd seen on television and in media images, this one wore a crown of jewels. He was enveloped in a dome of rainbows. He was bedecked in a bright red robe, studded with sparkling rubies and diamonds. He held, in one of his eight hands, a white-spotted red umbrella that looked like a mushroom. The scent of sandalwood filled the air around him.

The Dalai Lama gestured towards me, his eyes opening wide. Our eyes met.

"When you look at your ten-year-old son, Travis, do you see every single moment of his being?" His eyebrows arching while he spoke.

I was surprised he knew my son's name. "What do you mean?" I asked.

"Which version of him is true?" he replied, holding his hands in a prayer. When he stopped speaking, I noticed he was reciting a prayer to himself. He had a slight smile on his face.

When I didn't speak, he clarified.

"Is it the moment he was born, or his present state of being ten? Or is he always becoming? Like when you look at any object—are you seeing every instance, every permutation of that object? Take, for example, when you look at your wife's wedding ring. Do you see the millions of years it took to create the diamonds? Or do you see the history of the white gold on her ring? How the gold was mined from the ground. How it was separated from the other sediments. Do you imagine the instruments used? The labor it took? The life of each worker, from birth to death? How it was transported from one location to another? Do you see the gold, or the diamond, at the atomic level? Or, going smaller, at the subatomic level? Which version of the ring do you see? Or do you see them all?"

I didn't have an answer. My mind raced thinking about the onslaught of questions. As I contemplated his queries, the Dalai Lama's face morphed into my mother's face. This made me soften. He smiled my mother's smile. Her skin was young, unwrinkled. She was happy. I had forgotten how much I had missed that smile. Her smile said, *I'm looking out for you. I love you and will always put you first.* I felt her love wash over me.

Then his face changed again. Now he looked like Peter Rowan. Peter winked. Then he was Harry Smith. Next, me as a baby. Then Yungchen Lhamo. The transformations sped up until they happened every tenth of a second. I even saw the faces of monkeys and reptiles. Then the transformations stopped.

Now I was in a tall building, climbing up stairs. The building reminded me of abandoned factories I'd hung out in as a kid. There were many people milling about, climbing stairs, bumping into each other. Shaking my head, trying to compose myself, I slowly scaled up one flight of steps. I somehow knew that each rung led to different times, different places. Looking at the faces of the people around me, I noticed that they all were emanations of me.

I sighed, then all the faces sighed in unison. I yawned and they all yawned. We were caught in a moment when the paths and places of the universe—the multiverse—were revealed. Like I was staring into walls of reflecting mirrors.

The mirrors folded into a single diamond. Above the gem's multifaceted surface was a shimmering pink glow. I instinctively understood that the diamond would enable me to travel across galaxies, worming through time and space. I could see different periods and places on various facets of the diamond. On one facet, I saw a young Peter Rowan sitting on his porch alone. Looking across the meadow from his house, he watched the flickering lights of a carnival in town. I could hear a calliope in the distance. I felt Peter's loneliness, the yearning in his soul. I felt his heart pumping, his blood rush through his veins. I called out to him across the walls of time. He looked up but didn't see anything.

In another facet, I saw a young Bill Monroe, with his Uncle Pen, on a moonlight hayride, racing across the rolling hills of Rosine, Kentucky. The white of the moon streaked across the dark of the night like a broken egg. I heard Bill Monroe and Uncle Pen howling, hooting, and laughing.

In yet another facet, I saw a bodhi tree, surrounded by a clear blue sky. The tree gently waved in the wind. The tree's motion slowly increased. Now swaying hypnotically, its branches curled like snakes. I could hear a song emerging from inside the tree, as if from its inner soul. The song was deeply moving. I couldn't understand the words, but I knew the feelings it conveyed. Like a million saints sweetly singing, the song's melody told the stories of people's lives, their sadnesses and joys. Tears ran down my face. Like the great Mother who loves us all, the tree loved me. Her song told me that she was here for all beings. The tree didn't expect to be heard or understood in a commonsense manner. She spoke across eons. To piece together her message, you had to listen for centuries upon centuries.

The tree's honeyed tune took me on a journey. I was now beneath the ground, traversing the vast mycorrhizal network below it. I could hear animal noises. And the sounds of insect mandibles scraping against each other. I could even make out the delicate sound of plants unfolding. As if from miles away, I heard a sparrow delicately drinking water from a river. Moving at the speed of light, I witnessed the decomposition of animal skulls, ancient tree trunks, oak, ash and pine, and even buried boulders. As the white foam of decay swarmed over them, I saw new life sprout. Delicate birds alighted on the newly sprung ocotillo plants,[5] drinking nectar from them. There was a profusion of birdsong. The air was drunk with the fragrance of piñon.

This vision evaporated.

The Dalai Lama sat by the bodhi tree in a lotus position. The facets folded back up into a shimmering diamond and everything stilled for one long moment. Then, in one spectacular second, the diamond shattered. Pieces of history floated around me, like asteroids. I envisioned a homeless old man, who looked like my father, dying alone on a bench, hungry. I could feel his hunger in the pit of my stomach. A female Neanderthal, her eyes moist and red, slowly bleeding to death from a wound made by a tiger. Her breath was deep and hot. I heard cries muffled in her chest. I saw beings that didn't look like me but were me. Fish, birds, souls that looked like radio waves.

The building and stairs vanished.

Now only the Dalai Lama remained, holding his hands in prayer, chanting without opening his mouth. His chanting was thunderous. I could hear chainsaws, lawnmowers, trucks, and the groan of dying stars in its drone. It echoed throughout a billion universes.

Presenting a holographic rainbow triangle on his palm, the Dalai Lama then chanted into the triangle. Like an alchemist's magical instrument, the triangle transformed the chanting into birdsong, revealing its holiness. I realized or recognized that the tree's music, the birdsong, and the chant were all the same.

The rainbow triangle exploded with a flash of lightning bolts that struck the ground next to me. The Dalai Lama was now draped in a white banner.

"Practice charity without holding in mind any conception of charity, for charity is after all just a word," he said.

Now the Dalai Lama was sitting high atop a winged white horse, which appeared out of nowhere. The horse dashed away, the Dalai Lama's banner flapping in the wind behind him. I watched the Dalai Lama slowly disappear into a swirling cloud of red mist in the distance.

It is possible that the next Buddha will not take the form of an individual. The next Buddha may take the form of a community — a community practicing understanding and loving kindness, a community practicing mindful living. This may be the most important thing we can do for the survival of the earth. — Thich Nhat Hanh

Cure yourself with the light of the sun and the rays of the moon.
With the sound of the river and the waterfall.
With the swaying of the sea and the fluttering of birds.
Heal yourself with mint, with neem and eucalyptus.
Sweeten yourself with lavender, rosemary, and chamomile.
Hug yourself with the cocoa bean and a touch of cinnamon.
Put love in tea instead of sugar and take it looking at the stars.
Heal yourself with the kisses that the wind gives you and the hugs of the rain.
Get strong with bare feet on the ground and with everything that is born from it.
Get smarter every day by listening to your intuition, looking at the world with the eye of your forehead.
Jump, dance, sing, so that you live happier.
Heal yourself, with beautiful love, and always remember: you are the medicine.
—María Sabina

To rush headlong into the comforting darkness of selfhood as a reborn human being, or even as a beast, an unhappy ghost, a denizen of hell. Anything rather than the burning brightness of unmitigated Reality.
—Aldous Huxley, *The Doors of Perception*

A Little Aside from the Lore of Seventh Century Buddhism

Padmasambhava, the lotus-born Indian mystic, is, after Buddha Shakyamuni, the most important figure in the Tibetan Buddhist tradition.[6] Padmasambhava journeyed across the Himalayan Mountains in the ninth century, bringing Buddhism to Tibet. It is said that he lived in India for one thousand years and remained in Tibet for one hundred twenty years.

Padmasambhava was not an ordinary being. His magical powers, however, were used solely for the benefit of all beings. Along his journey, he encountered many wicked spirits and demons. In miraculous victory after victory, he conquered evil kings, rakshasas, dakinis, and other malevolent beings. During his voyage, he sometimes disguised himself as a homeless man, or a sorceress, and other identities. On one occasion he metamorphosed into a boulder for centuries and remained that way to avoid a battle with an evil magician. Sometimes it wasn't necessary to confront evil directly, he learned. But Padmasambhava also summoned meteors from the sky to fling at his enemies. He could tip the earth to cause floods. And he could wield hail and lightning.

Like Shakyamuni, Padmasambhava was an emanation of all Buddhas. He came to this world to offer salvation through his teachings, to be like the "moonlight of compassion on the lake of his disciple's faith."

When Padmasambhava was about to leave Tibet, he was accompanied by his retinue. At the border of Nepal, he was escorted by dakinis on a horse called Mahabala. Some say the white horse Mahabala was also known as Mescalito, but this was never written down. It was whispered lips to lips over the centuries. As he flew away on Mescalito's back, his banner flapping in the wind, Padmasambhava's disciples watched his image slowly getting smaller and smaller, eventually disappearing into a red mist.

Padmasambhava now gone, a flock of blue scrub jays erupted from the sky, flying to the four corners of the earth.

And Who is Mescalito?

Student: Who is Mescalito? Is he the horse?

Padmasambhava: Sometimes he's the horse and sometimes he's riding the horse.

Student: I'm confused. How can he be both?

Padmasambhava: Mescalito is the protector.

Student: How does Mescalito protect?

Padmasambhava: He advises. He answers questions.

Student: Is Mescalito real? Can I see him?

Padmasambhava: Mescalito is in your dreams, your intuitions. While you chase illusions, pictures projected on a screen, Mescalito is the source of what is real.

Student: How do I know what is real?

Padmasambhava: It is only through the emptiness of awareness that we know what is real.

Student: How can I know emptiness?

Padmasambhava: Breathe.

Student: Breathing is all?

Padmasambhava: Breathe with your heart. See the world through your heart.

Student: Can someone teach me?

Padmasambhava: When the student is ready, the Buddha will appear.

Midnight Moonlight[7]

I've always known Peter Rowan. We've been crossing paths in the multiverse for billions of years, traversing the mysterious wormhole transportation system, dancing illusion's dance, singing illusion's song. *Voices crying in the wilderness.*[8] On a few occasions we've made contact. Like the time I was a cat being born in Peter's backyard in 1947, to help him recall the cycle of life. He was five years old. After seeing the cat being born, wandering around the farmyard near his house, Peter heard voices calling him from deep inside the earth, songs of moss and fungi, sung like prayers. As he bent down to touch the moist loam, he heard the rain dripping through the canopy of trees overhead. Even the delicate breeze delivering the dank smell of mycelium across the field remains in his memory. But it was the cat that awakened his sense of the cycle of life. And I was the cat.

Years later, singing at his father's funeral with his brothers, awash with the scent of the freshly turned soil, this old memory came back to him. *There in the earth, all things return,* he mused. *Down in the dark soil, transformation and rebirth occur. Though unthought of and invisible to most people, the fungi silently connect everything to everything, breaking down organic matter, transforming it to base elements, binding all living and nonliving matter in a wreath. At different points in time, all phenomena play musical chairs. We are sometimes the cat, the scrub jay, the fungi, the soil, the wind. Or our mother, our father. Or the Buddha.*

Only in the future would Peter think back to that moment and recall that he was contemplating the circularity of existence.

I encountered another emanation of Peter when I heard him singing "Midnight Moonlight" on the *Old & In the Way* album in 1981. I was fifteen. As the trains clanged overhead on that winter night, Johnny Squid and I huddled in the stairwell of a factory building in Queens Plaza in New York City. Peter's voice, playing on a cassette recorder, called me from the future, ricocheting off the steel walls of the factory. In that moment, Squid and I were living through centuries, millennia, even eons. Peter's singing told the story of the woes and longings of humanity, from even before we stood upright and walked the plains. His voice transported us back to a time before there was an earth. We saw the place where God dwelled.

Like God, this book has no beginning or end. It existed before it was written.

I met Peter again, in essence, when Yungchen Lhamo met Ernie Paniccioli. This is an epic moment, like when a galaxy coalesces, or when a star collapses into a black hole.

Winding through a crowd of famous stars and musicians at a Philip Glass performance, having never seen him before, Yungchen walked up to Ernie and started touching his face.

Ernie was stunned.

The room fell silent.

"He looks like someone in my family," she said, drinking in Ernie's eyes. They held hands like they'd always known each other.

Then, when I met Yungchen, talking to her via FaceTime, she silently mouthed Tibetan prayers and held prayer beads. She was dressed in blue and red traditional Tibetan silk clothing. Her hair was wrapped up in a bun, a blue coral dangling from atop her bun. She was beautiful. The wall behind her was draped with Tibetan tankas.

I asked Yungchen about playing bluegrass with Peter, which I had read about in an article online.

"Would you like to talk to him?"

"Of course, I would."

After our FaceTime call, she texted me his number.

He's waiting for you to call, she wrote.

Like we were delivered to each other. It was no mistake that Peter Rowan and I connected in this cycle of life, too.

I was incredibly nervous. I called him, stuttering and wincing.

"What do you want to talk about?" he asked. He sounded a little impatient but not rude. He was driving. I could imagine him thinking, *Who is this person that Yungchen asked me to speak to?* I had called him out of the blue. It was a fair question.

"Your career. The spirituality of bluegrass?" As I spoke, I held the phone away from my face, thinking, *How stupid I must sound.*

"The spiritual aspects of music. Okay. I got it," he said, now sounding more relaxed. He knew just what I meant, it seemed.

"Let's talk tomorrow," he said. We arranged a time to speak.

A few days later after our initial call, I woke up early in the morning and read an e-mail on my phone from Peter. *I'm enjoying your tales*, he said, referring to my book *Falling from Trees*, which I'd sent him. "I have to share with you a poem I wrote called 'Falling from Trees,'" he added. How could that be? How could we have written something with the same title? There was something afoot here. I put my phone down and went back to sleep.

At this point, I began having conversations in my head with Peter. And he occupied my dreams. There was an uncanny communication happening between us. Perhaps he had taken shamanic possession of me. Or was I just imagining this? Or both?

After a few weeks, I sent him an early draft of the article I was writing. It was a conversational interview, offering the reader a chronology of Peter's career. The article wasn't a work of literature.

We exchanged iterations of the article as I drafted revisions. Peter corrected some of the facts I'd written down. One was a quote I'd scribbled about Bill Monroe. I'd asked Peter what he learned from playing with Monroe. I had written: *Everyone played to the rhythm of Monroe's voice.* Peter corrected it, writing: *Everyone playing to Bill Monroe's impeccable mandolin rhythm and tenor voice.*

Peter also said that he didn't refer to his players by last names as I had done. Bill Monroe and Bill Keith needed full names, not just last names to distinguish them. This little bit says a lot about who Peter is and how he views his musician friends. The fact that he's played with many of the same people most of his life says a lot about who he is, too.

Peter's melodies and song lyrics had invaded my being. I was connected to Peter through my thoughts and dreams. In one dream I beheld a vision of a previous life: I was Casey Jones, conductor of the Intergalactic Hayride Association. As conductor it was my job to help beings navigate bardo. Maybe they'd slipped and cracked their head or died suddenly in a violent car crash. Or, like Aldous Huxley, they died slowly listening to *The Tibetan Book of the Dead* being read to them. In all cases, I was the guide. The journey after death for all was determined by the life of the person who had died.

The next night I dreamt of meeting Peter.

"Hi Peter," I said.

"Who are you?" he asked.

"*It ain't the who, it's the what,*" I replied.

We both started laughing. He remembered he knew me. But he couldn't remember where he knew me from.

"I was the cat in your backyard," I said.

He smiled knowingly.

Then, laughing, I added, "I am the walrus."

We were both hysterical for almost a full minute.

Peter's eyes suddenly narrowed. He stopped laughing.

"We've always had this dream," he whispered. "The dream continues to dream us and dream itself."[9] Then he smiled again and winked at me. His lips moved as he prayed to himself.

That night I had a million dreams, like a million suns being born and dying. In one fantastic vision I was a pathetic fool, asking stupid questions, feeling like a fraud.

"What is the nature of reality?" I said.

"That's such a silly question," a voice replied.

"Isn't that the first question?"

"Just breathe. Breathe from your heart," the voice replied.

In another dream, I was a learned sage who had complete mastery over my body. I taught my disciples how to control their breathing. How to fast. How to tolerate extreme cold and heat.

It was as if the dreams were dialed into my mind by Peter.

In one dream Peter was my student.

"What is the nature of reality?" Peter asked.

"Reality is imagined," I replied. Peter closed his eyes and fell into a deep meditation.

In another dream, I was Peter's disciple. As I sat in the center of a small room on the floor, Peter danced around me, chanting, daintily dropping lotus pedals from his fingers.

"And now I'm going to give you your mantra," said Peter.

He stopped dancing, folded his hands to his chest and began whispering a prayer.

"I am looking into Rama's mouth to find your mantra," he said, praying to himself between each spoken word.

I looked up at him, awaiting his next word.

"And now, I have your mantra," said Peter after a minute or two of silence. "This ancient mantra has been selected for you. Bestowed upon you out of thousands of other mantras."

I closed my eyes now.

"Your mantra is ..." said Peter, pausing. "Your mantra is *shiring*."

Then we began chanting *shiring* together. Our chanting became loud, our voices like a room full of lawnmowers turned on. Our bodies lifted off the floor of the room. We were levitating together, swimming around the room, pushing off the ceiling, like two balloons. Now we dissolved into a red midst, transitioning between worlds, like shadows, sometimes even being each other for a fleeting instant. When Peter's being moved through my soul, I was flooded with his memories. I pictured Peter picking up the mandolin for the first time, plucking it clumsily, trying to voice out the melody to "Blue Moon of Kentucky."

The next day I prepared for my call with Peter, getting my questions ready. I played his albums, discovering ones I hadn't heard previously. I listened to his *Dharma Blues* album, which featured songs like "Wisdom Woman" and "My Love Will Never Change." I remembered that Peter was a Buddhist. Why did I not recall that when Yungchen introduced me to him? Funny how that works, I thought. Our being becomes so entangled in experience that it forgets itself.[10] I thought about how Aldous Huxley's book *Island* opens with the word *attention* repeated, calling to mind the notion that to achieve awareness of ourselves and our reality in every moment, we must practice the art of being awake. Even the word *Buddha* means awake. Awake. Arise! Clap, clap, clap! Wake up. Wake up. In Tibetan dream yoga, practitioners remain awake even when sleeping. The goal is to remain awake, always. In the West we call this lucid dreaming. The practice of staying awake is well-known in Tibetan Buddhist, Bön (Tibet's pre-Buddhist religion), and some Native American and other Indigenous spiritual traditions.

Arise. Awake. Awake!

Clap!

When Peter and I spoke on the phone for our interview, it was like two old friends catching up. *I've always known you, Peter*, I wanted to say. We talked about his music, his time with Bill Monroe, playing with the great bluegrass players. Talking to Peter was like reminiscing. And, of course, our lives were shared, though sometimes across opposite sides of the vinyl.

While Peter played the songs, unleashing the power of the ancient tones, like Krishna playing his flute to the stars, I was gorged with inspiration. Like thousands of other people. It took me years to "hear" the deeper messages in the songs. It occurred to me, after many deep listenings, that Peter had to conceal the potency of this knowledge. Like the magical powers of Padmasambhava teachings, the meditations and prayers could be used for either bad or good purposes. Peter learned from Padmasambhava that, without compassion, a practitioner can be led astray. The mind can create entire universes and destroy them, too. If not nourished properly, wisdom can transform from a beneficial tool to a blunted weapon.

After our call, when I went to sleep that night, the dream visions continued. Now I looked forward to going to sleep, knowing that I'd see Peter.

In one, I was at a concert dancing with Eric Dolphy and Patsy Cline. Otis Redding played guitar and sang. There were other people there too, some of whom I didn't know.

Something amazing had happened. Humans had made contact with highly intelligent beings from another world. As if in an instant, these beings taught us how to live more just lives. How to protect every human being. How to acknowledge the sovereignty of trees, oceans, and rivers.

We were celebrating our liberation.

There were three suns in this world. A giant red planet hung in the sky visibly, as if leaning into the surface of the planet.

I heard music coming from the stage. When I looked up, it was Peter Rowan playing with Bill Monroe, Jerry Garcia, and Patsy Cline. At the front of the stage sat Padmasambhava and Yungchen Lhamo (or was it Yeshe Tsogyal?).

I later realized that I had been dreaming of Peter's song "On the Blue Horizon." The song tells of the return of an age of greatness. A time when the great creatives like Eric Dolphy, John Coltrane, and Patsy Cline return. A time when all people come together to fight for each other's freedom. This song symbolizes much of what Peter Rowan has meant to me. Someone who has dug a tunnel connecting the old and the new, the ancient tones and holy singing of bluegrass with the New Age tones of psychedelia.

After Peter played, he came down from the stage chanting: Freedom for us is a prison for the rulers of might.[11]

> We greeted each other and embraced. I cried tears of happiness.
> If you ever feel lonesome,
> And you're down in San Antone,
> Beg, steal, or borrow two nickels or a dime,
> And call me on the phone.
> I'll meet you at Alamo mission,
> And we can say our prayers,
> The Holy Ghost and the Virgin Mother
> Will heal us as we kneel there.
> In the moonlight, in the midnight,
> In the moonlight, midnight moonlight.
> If you ever feel sorrow for the deeds you have done,
> With no hope for tomorrow in the setting of the sun.
> And the ocean is howling of things that might have been,
> And that last good morning sunrise
> Will be the brightest you've ever seen.
> In the moonlight, in the midnight,
> In the moonlight, midnight moonlight.
> —"Midnight Moonlight" (*Peter Rowan*, Peter Rowan)

The other four aspects of human existence—
feeling, thought, will, and consciousness—
are likewise nothing more than emptiness,
and emptiness nothing more than they.
All things are empty:

Nothing is born, nothing dies,
nothing is pure, nothing is stained,
nothing increases and nothing decreases.
So, in emptiness, there is no body,
no feeling, no thought,
no will, no consciousness.
There are no eyes, no ears,
no nose, no tongue,
no body, no mind.
There is no seeing, no hearing,
no smelling, no tasting,
no touching, no imagining.
There is nothing seen, nor heard,
nor smelled, nor tasted,
nor touched, nor imagined.
There is no ignorance,
and no end to ignorance.
There is no old age and death,
and no end to old age and death.
There is no suffering, no cause of suffering,
no end to suffering, no path to follow.
There is no attainment of wisdom,
and no wisdom to attain.
The Bodhisattvas rely on the Perfection of Wisdom,
and so with no delusions,
they feel no fear,
and have Nirvana here and now.
All the Buddhas,
past, present, and future,
rely on the Perfection of Wisdom,
and live in full enlightenment.
The Perfection of Wisdom is the greatest mantra.
It is the clearest mantra,
the highest mantra,

the mantra that removes all suffering.
This is truth that cannot be doubted.
—"The Heart Sutra"

Who Will Live Will Love[12]

Throughout the months after I first talked to Peter, I continued having intense dreams. I dreamed that I was Peter and he was me. We lived each other's lives—every single moment, waking and sleeping. One moment I was in the car with Bill Monroe, driving to a gig. He pulled over to the side of the road to sing the melody to "Walls of Time," then asked me to remember the song and write the lyrics. Monroe telling me to *sing like Peter Roans* ("Roans" was how Monroe said "Rowan"). To not try to imitate him or anyone else. And then there was Peter growing up in Long Island City, smoking pot in the stairwells of factory buildings on Northern Boulevard near Queens Plaza. The trains roared by on cold winter nights as Johnny Squid and I played my *Old & In the Way* cassette tape. Echoing off the steel walls, the songs rang in his mind as if forged in cauldrons of fire.

As I lived Peter's last sixty years, feeling all its moments, thinking that perhaps his was the better life, more enriched, more achieved, I suddenly awoke to a bell ringing. Maybe Peter awoke at the same time. I had lived half a lifetime, every single dripping moment of it, but all in a few minutes. Still, those fifty years felt real. Every long night. Every moment of hopelessness. And of joy. The death of parents, the loss of friends. Perhaps Peter had dreamt my life. And in his dream of my life, he had discovered some wisdom, too. That all lives are just lives. All our lives are the same, even as they are different. Our sufferings unite us. Our victories are yet shared. His songs are my songs.

After the *Atwood Magazine* article was published, I felt a little sad, like our friendship was over. And I wasn't completely sure if Peter liked the article. I told him I wanted to write a longer piece. Something about how bluegrass created the universe, or how the universe created bluegrass. I had to get something down. There was so much more to be said. I just didn't know exactly what that was. You're reading what I wanted to say.

Mescalito Riding His White Horse

"I'll be heading out to the Bay Area," I wrote to Peter, months after we began speaking.

"Looking forward to meeting you," he wrote back. "Let's talk before you come to California." I suggested that we meet somewhere in Sausalito near where he lived.

I called him about a week before my arrival in California to work out the plan. As I started to talk, he said, "Hold on, hold on. Sorry, I'm in a bad cell area. I'm in the mountains, on my way to meet Peter Coyote and Ramblin' Jack Elliott."

They were working on a project, something that would get filmed. Upon hearing that, I felt struck by a thunderbolt. People are people. But here I was one degree away from some of the very minds who had created the consciousness in which I dwell. Peter Coyote and Ramblin' Jack Elliott, along with others like Jack Kerouac, Diane di Prima, Bobby Seale, Maybelle Carter, Lawrence Ferlinghetti, Martin Luther King Jr., and Allen Ginsberg exploded upon the postwar 1950s and gave us the music, the environmental awareness, the poetry, and the consciousness-expanding milieu in which I grew up. I was who I was because of their imaginations. Because of their resistance. And now I was holding a phone dialed into the vortex of that creative explosion. Like I was staring into Rama's mouth and saw the entire universe.

I followed them all out to the Bay Area in my twenties, after taking a cross-country trip with my friend Felicia. More than a friend, but never really a girlfriend, Felicia entered my life around 1981 when we went on a blind date.

My friend Chris said, "My girlfriend is coming back from camp with her friend and wants to go out. Would you be into that?"

I was open to the idea.

Chris had been a Black Sabbath metalhead a few years prior but had suddenly become a hippie, a devoted Deadhead who wore a knitted rainbow hat.

"She's cute," he added, so of course now I was interested.

That first night we all went out to see *The Rocky Horror Picture Show*. In the dark theater's balcony, Felicia and I were making out. Feeling each other up even as Chris sang out the call-and-response to the movie. We were completely into each other. Chris and his girlfriend couldn't believe how quickly Felicia and I had connected.

As the years went by, Felicia and I would be friends and sometimes lovers, depending on which of us was in a relationship at the time. We also shared many interests. Being from the suburbs, Felicia got a taste of the New York City projects from me. We made out in back hallways and on park benches in dark places in Long Island City. I was a kid from a tough neighborhood. I was muscular. Even a little dangerous for her. She was curious and I found her interesting, smart. When we weren't tearing each other's clothes off we were discussing philosophy and literature. I think she gave me my first copy of *Howl*.

We watched each other change over the years, but especially when we went to college. At New York University, still living at home and taking the train back and forth to school every day, I shed my tough guy clothes and looks. While at Tufts, Felicia stopped shaving her underarms. No more lipstick. Her hair wasn't as coiffed as it had once been. She was now a Deadhead. Instead of meeting in back hallways, we met at Lincoln Center.

When we graduated college, she asked me if I wanted to take a trip across the country with her. She had taken a job in Berkeley, California. I had never really been anywhere, so I said yes.

What does this have to do with Peter Rowan, you may be wondering? It has everything to do with Peter Rowan. Peter's spiritual force was the glue that kept Felicia and me in touch, even as we changed and evolved.

Our trip across the country was torn from a page in Kerouac's *On the Road*, which inspired Rowan's generation and Peter very directly. Even though he is a generation before me, we were drinking from the same well.

I moved out to the Bay Area around 1990 and stayed with Felicia for a few weeks in the Oakland hills, until I found a place in downtown Oakland. Prior to that, I had been living in my parents' home in Long Island City while attending college. Afterwards, I'd remained in Queens, living with a girlfriend. I had to escape the little fishbowl of my world.

After going out to California to scout opportunities, I found a job, packed all my things and left the girlfriend I had been living with. She was supposed to join me but decided not to in the end.

This was the first time I'd be living alone. Being on my own in a different state, I was worried that I'd go crazy. That I'd feel too lonely. But I didn't. I found myself. There were Buddhas holding me up the whole time.

I began going to meditation centers around the Bay Area. Since I worked in Berkeley, I walked to the Empty Gate Zen Center, which sat atop a small hill near the Berkeley campus. Having been raised Catholic, I could relate to the prayers and sacred objects of Catholicism but not its ideology. Meditating in the Empty Gate Zen Center was the first time I embraced a spiritual practice. I felt noble sitting on my mat meditating. I was good at it. I could meditate for forty-five minutes, reaching states of emptiness.

I also went to the San Francisco Zen Center, perched on a hill in the Haight-Ashbury district. I often drank coffee at one of my favorite cafés before going to the center. Smelling the beautiful fragrances of jasmine and eucalyptus while sipping my coffee, I beheld a beautiful vision of the city. Atop the rolling hills in the Haight, with the bay in view, San Francisco looked like a sparkling jewel. A jewel of priceless worth.[13] The San Francisco Zen Center was gigantic. The old wood floors creaked when you walked on them. I felt at home at the Zen Center. I could meditate there for long stretches. But what did it mean to be a good meditator?

At one point, nearly out of money, I talked to Steve, the director at the Empty Gate Zen Center. I had been practicing meditation and attending services at Empty Gate, but now I entertained the idea of moving into the center.

"You could live at the center for free," said Steve.

I was interested.

"Free room and board," he replied. "But," he added, the smile fading off his face, "you'll have to work at the center's hospice to take care of people who are basically coming here to die."

"To die?"

"They come here when the hospitals and doctors have given up. You care for them and feed them. You hold their hands."

I nodded.

"Do you think you can do this?" he asked, knowing this wasn't easy for anyone.

"Let me think it over," I said.

After mulling it over for a bit I decided not to move in. I didn't think I was strong enough to be that close to death. I hadn't yet achieved those levels of compassion or enough of an understanding of emptiness. My meditation skills meant only so much.

Broke, I moved back to New York City, only to face my own father's early death. For years I had a recurring dream that New York City and San Francisco were connected by a bridge. I could get to either place in a matter of minutes.

Interview with Peter Rowan in Sausalito

In the days leading up to the meeting with Peter in the Bay Area, I texted him saying that I'd lived out there too, twenty-five years ago. I added, "All my changes were there," quoting Neil Young, even though that sounded a little corny.

This time I wasn't going to interview Peter. I intended to have an extended philosophical conversation about the origins of music. I was inspired by a YouTube video interview posted by Christopher Henry. A former Bluegrass Boy in Peter's band, Christopher went all the way: inviting Peter to open up and extemporize on his ideas about nature, spirituality, and the origins of music. This is the direction I wanted my follow-up writing project to take.

I wanted to ask Peter about Kerouac's influence on his writing and his vision but decided it would be off topic. I wrote down a few other notes to myself:

Aldous Huxley
Robin Wall Kimmerer (Indigenous botanist, author of *Braiding Sweetgrass*)
Cowboy Buddha

"I'm going to ask him questions about the origins of music," I told my wife, Arielle, when she asked what I was planning.

"Isn't that a bit far out?" said Arielle.

"Peter's a poet. He can talk about *anything*. I'm interested in *the what of the what*."

Arielle giggled at me. But she knows that when I get into something, I go all the way.

"You'll figure it out," she added.

From my Airbnb in Oakland, I exchanged text messages with Peter the day I was to meet him.

"How are you getting here?" he wrote. "You have to be careful not to run into traffic." I was touched that he considered my journey to see him.

When I drove into Sausalito on June 1, 2021, one day before my birthday, the sun was shining brightly. I passed yoga studios, meditation and wellness centers, Tibetan restaurants, and many colorful multi-million-dollar homes. Sausalito is like nirvana for wealthy people. They have money, but they also seem to be striving for a higher consciousness, for a more meaningful life.

I looked across the road and saw Peter emerging from a white SUV. *Mescalito Riding His White Horse.* Donning a white Stetson hat, Peter slowly walked across the street to where I was waiting at Sartaj India Café. He was wearing sandals. Standing about six foot two, he looked like a jovial cowboy Buddha with his protruding belly. His white wispy hair was piled like cotton on his head. He walked like it hurt him to move. Like his knees were weakened.

I stood and we shook hands. "So great to meet you," I said.

Almost immediately, we were talking and joking as if we'd always known each other. Like he knew me just as much as I knew him from his records and lyrics. We talked about Brooklyn and how his daughter Amanda had lived there when she went to graduate school at New York University. And about his sons, Michael, John and Elijah. I talked about my two sons, Thelonious and Travis. I performed my Brooklyn Shakespeare for Peter, reciting Hamlet's "To be, or not to be" speech in a Brooklyn accent, which was met with Peter's laughter.

After the waiter brought our food, Peter pushed his order of vegetable momo toward me. And I offered my bowl of dal makhani to him. I liked that we shared bowls, like we were mixing our essences. The food was delicious.

When the check came, Peter grabbed it. "No, please," I said. "I invited you." We gently fought about it, but Peter eventually yielded to my plea to pay for lunch.

"Let's go somewhere to continue our conversation," I said.

"I'm getting work done in my house," said Peter.

"I just need a place where I can record the conversation. Somewhere quiet."

We went to a café with an outdoor area where we could talk and I could record. I placed my iPhone in the cradle I'd brought with me and we got started.

"How did you get interested in Buddhism?" I asked.

"There was a time I experienced a feeling of, 'It ain't the what of the what you think you think you're thinking but it's the where of the what of what you think you're thinking.'"

We both laughed.

"That's my answer," he said. But then he pulled himself up to a more erect sitting position and continued.

"As a kid I felt a presence. But my first experience was watching a cat give birth in our kitchen. I was about four years old. It struck me of this sense of something being born. 'Where did it come from?' I asked my mother, 'Where are we before we're born?' And my mother said, 'You're in your mother's tummy before you're born.'

"Then, when I was five, I decided to go exploring, for which I was punished. I wandered into the meadow behind our house. I was beyond the boundaries of where I was allowed to be. We lived in my father's grandfather's house in the country. I wandered down and crossed the stream we called the brook. When they realized I was missing, my mother came after me, dragged me home, and spanked me with a hairbrush. The good ol' corporal punishment days. But then I became habituated to taking solitary walks. When my brother Chris was born, I was suddenly free. I started wandering and exploring. My connecting to these philosophies was an extension of these explorations of the natural world. Because in the country, we go out in the fall, winter, spring, and summer and see the same patch of bushes or cattails by the stream, but they're all changing. I had that sense of change, of seasons and growth. And the area that I grew up in was a farming town. My family had a relationship with one of the farmers. I did menial work for him. I think it came from a sense of *What is this* that seeing life on a farm can inspire. And a sense of wonder. As that sense arises in the natural world, you kind of get an answer. I couldn't articulate it at the time. Then I took communion and got baptized. The power of prayers as a young child. Then as a teenager you fall in love. You discover passion and that the world is a wonderful place. The person that you love, you love more than your parents. You love more than anything you've ever experienced. And you feel transported. And then around twelve years old, I started to play music publicly at local CYO dances. Along with the music rising as an inspiring expression of everything that happens to every teenager."

"At some point did you read Buddhist texts?" I asked.

"Not necessarily about Buddhism, but I began to learn about where I lived. The area between Concord, Lexington, Wayland in Massachusetts. Walden Pond is there. That's where Thoreau lived and these countercultural figures of his time. I began to get interested in the history and learn about it. The feeling was in the air. From Thoreau, I found my way to Hemingway, and then to Kerouac, who was also a New Englander. To think that he didn't speak English until he was seven or eight years old. Then I started looking for the texts that reflected what Kerouac and Thoreau were writing about. I eventually read *On the Road* which was a perfect portrayal of the America I was born into and grew up in."

"Have you read it recently?" I asked.

"I'm reading it now," said Peter.

Hearing that his readings on Buddhism led him to Jack Kerouac sent a chill up my spine, the synchronicity like a live wire almost on fire with sparks. This is what I mean when I say Peter had everything to do with my move out west.

"I'm reading the unedited manuscript," he continued. "The original book is a little tighter. As soon I was seventeen or eighteen, I went on the road across the country with a friend of mine. I read Kerouac and then the world was that place. And then there was the folk music scene that was starting up. Playing high school record hops with my band, the Cupids. Then there was the coffee house scene. But I didn't go the coffee house route. I would go hear music at coffee houses, but I went to see music there because people like Muddy Waters and the great Clarence White and the Kentucky Colonels played there. But my access to the blues was through the music of Bill Monroe. That is where I started to get a sense of lineage. Here's somebody who played before me, and before him there was another person and so on. And the music sounded different because of each person's contribution. Then I went to Nashville, Tennessee, when I was twenty-two. I stayed there until I was twenty-four. I left Nashville and Bill Monroe when I was twenty-six to form Earth Opera with David Grisman. We were open to Taoist thought, free jazz, and I was studying Aristotle. I discovered the Greek word meaning *to know*. Of course, in the sixties, we were asking what is it *to know*? How do you know something? It turns out in the writings of Aristotle, which were kept alive by the Sufi thinkers of the twelfth century, you had an entire system of codification of knowledge, which included Buddhist concepts. Buddhist syllogisms were chanted aloud. What this did was use up all the logical formulations of the mind and free it into a state of Gnostic awareness. My teacher at the time told me that nowadays science is very particular, but previously science was a part of religious thinking. One of the existing systems of thought which included science in its core thinking is Tibetan Buddhism.

"My father had a book by his bed called *Out of This World: Across the Himalayas to Forbidden Tibet* by Lowell Thomas. That book was a journalist's view of hidden Tibet. During this time,

I was beginning to get messages from the beyond. It turned out to be Amitabha Buddha, the red Buddha. We were living down on the Plymouth Plantation on the edge of Cape Cod. This was about 1968. I was living with my friend Dick Martin who studied with Richard Evans Schultes. Schultes had lived in the Amazon and wrote about the various hallucinogenic plants he discovered there. I then went to Tail of the Tiger in Vermont and studied with Chögyam Trungpa tulku, who started the Shambhala Institute. He was the eleventh Trungpa. Once you get into that kind of training, you're being trained to be a future Buddha. I remember one of the teachers, Kalu Rinpoche, said to me, *It's no mistake that you're here. This is from a previous connection.* This whole notion of previous connections and other lives added to the widening circle of awareness of what really is."

I then mentioned Aldous Huxley's final novel *Island*, in which Huxley creates a vision of utopia that was the very antithesis of his dystopian *Brave New World*. The fictitious Pacific Island of Pala is an "oasis of happiness and freedom," where for 120 years the inhabitants have resisted the trappings of capitalism, consumerism, and technology. In the story, the people on this island have developed a miraculous fusion of scientific thinking and spirituality. The story ends tragically, but Huxley gave us a vision of hope, of what could be.

"Didn't Aldous Huxley write *The Doors of Perception*?" asked Peter.

I answered affirmatively.

"Earth Opera had been touring with the Doors, after the Bill Monroe period. Jim Morrison really inspired me. We toured a lot with the Doors. Jim's playfulness and menace! It freed me to perform my song 'The Great American Eagle Tragedy' on another level.

"Backstage with the Doors, they were very professional. Before they became popular, they had played for two years at the Whisky a Go Go. They got their act together. They knew what their act was. They knew what to do. You go for that kind of discipline, and you will coalesce as an act. This was completely unlike Earth Opera. The producers were trying to get us to come together, to package our music for more commercial success, but we passed on that offer. In the end, we were a rough and ready little group. Bluegrass players playing rock 'n' roll. But the idea of relating to an audience, Jim had them eating out of his hands."

"In one interview," I said, "the interviewer asked you, 'What was it like to go from playing bluegrass to playing in a psychedelic band?' And your answer was, 'What could be more psychedelic than bluegrass?' I loved that answer. Can you tell me what you meant by this?"

"The veil that keeps bluegrass from being appreciated more deeply is that the notes go by too fast. The fiddle was the only sustaining instrument in a bluegrass ensemble. The guitar has occasional leads, but is mostly rhythm, hidden down in the matrix of counter-rhythms. When it worked it was transportive. Bluegrass is extremely hard to play to its true potential. I've heard tapes of Bill Monroe shows where the band wasn't up to it. That didn't stop Bill Monroe. The band could be dragging behind, but Bill wouldn't let them drag behind. One of the first things he told me before I joined the band and one of the last things he said was: 'Pete, I could take on all of the Bluegrass Boys and they couldn't wrastle me to the ground. I'd have them hanging off me like hound dogs off a grizzly bear. And they couldn't pull me down, man. Not even Gordon Terry. And he was stout.' That's a quote. If your ear was quick enough to hear beyond the beat. For instance, this Black woman was driving me to the airport one time. I asked her what she did. She showed me a briefcase she kept in the car. 'I'm working on a book. I'm going to tell it like it is. What's it's like to be a woman right now. To be a Black woman at that.' She was moonlighting, driving a car with her notebook right under the seat. 'And what do you do?' I told her I play bluegrass. 'That is the most uplifting music.' If you hear the emotional uplift, the message is a happy one. Imagine how burdened some people can be. It might be factory workers in Ohio or Kentucky that go to a bar or a pub to get that uplift. People come to different music for different things. It took me fifty years to appreciate that. People don't come to bluegrass to hear drums. You can put drums in there, it may mean something musically to the players, but it's not going to mean anything to the audience. That's not why the audience comes."

"The Osbornes used drums in their recordings," I said.

"But people still come to see the Osbornes for the harmonies, for fiddle playing, for the banjo playing. It's not an organic thing. To add drums to bluegrass it must be played with the same kind of roots that the instruments are played with. We had a drummer who could do it. Jamie Oldaker."

"Clapton's drummer?"

"Yes, Clapton's drummer. He was with us for the last three years."

He paused.

"Where was I going with that? Except to say that the psychedelia of bluegrass is almost microscopic. Normal humans can't hear the depth of bluegrass up front. It's not like you're playing two notes on a guitar that have sustain and you can hear the harmonics. In bluegrass the harmonics are on a higher level. In a way it's kind of a higher-level Pythagorean theory. It's going by very fast. And the long-sustained fiddle and the long vocal sustains, and vocal harmonies is what I loved about bluegrass. You take a blues and sing a two-part harmony. The song 'In the Pines.' That gave me chill-bumps. The elements in bluegrass that are psychedelic are like these dissonant chords like where Bill Monroe would sing in G and go to C and in the harmony in the C chord somebody would sing in F. People of my generation heard that, and we realized that Bill Monroe's dissonances were like John Coltrane's explorations."

"I felt that the three-dimensionality of bluegrass is what's psychedelic," I said. "If you're in a very receptive state, like being high on weed. You can hear the harmonies and counterpoints rise off the record." In *Earl Scruggs and the Foggy Mountain Boys*, Thomas Goldsmith quoted Ricky Skaggs saying that although bluegrass music is considered traditional today, it was so revolutionary in its time that it "sounded like a computer."

"What you're saying is that it ain't the what of the what of what you think you're thinking. But it's the where," Peter said.

We both chuckled.

"Let me tell you a story," I said. "When I worked in Berkeley, California, about thirty years ago, I loaned a Stanley Brothers tape to a friend. I think it was a live recording of the Stanley Brothers in the Shenandoah Valley. They gave it back to me and said, 'Why are you into this Christian gospel music?' And I replied, 'But did you listen to the music?' What do you think of that?"

A great wind blew into the courtyard where we sat. The air was cool and fresh.

Without skipping a beat, Peter replied.

"My answer to that question is long-standing. Spiritual music is spiritual music. There are not permanent names for anything," said Peter, laughing. *"It ain't the why of the what, it's the where of the why,"* he added. "Let's just say this, adherence to any code or faith is always going to be turned on by the words they associate with the feelings they have about their belief. But when you hear the Stanley Brothers singing 'The Angel of Death' or 'Standing at the Gate by My Savior's Right Hand,' it doesn't matter. Christians will hear that, and they understand it. But on a higher level that stuff is just spiritual music. You could be anybody in the world and get that feeling, which is part of the magic. I didn't find the gospel tunes primarily religious in my association with them, but 'I Saw the Light' was a great song to sing every night. And 'The Boat of Love' — 'Oh the boat of love down at the harbor, it's waiting there, for you and me. I have no fear Christ is the captain, he'll guide us o'er life's rollin' sea.' Everybody knows what the rolling sea is to some degree. Religion is the great masquerade people use for their own purposes. The study of Buddhism, if it can be accessible, requires that you go to it. It's not going to come and grab you. But once you have an experience of illumination that's beyond sectarian words or ideas, that's where spirituality dwells. But who knows, maybe the times are so materialistic that you need psychedelics. There's a song we did as a gospel tune that's a peyote chant."

Then Peter started singing, "I'm going up on the mountain, I ain't coming down till the morning. I'm going up on the mountain, I ain't coming down till day. I'm going up to set my soul free, I ain't coming down till the morning. I'm going up to set my soul free, I ain't coming down in chains. My savior lives inside of me, all I got to do is set him free. I ain't coming down in chains.

"That's a peyote song that Jody Stecher's cousin made into a gospel tune. He got it off a Smithsonian record. But to me that's a deeply spiritual song," Peter said. Here we had to pause the conversation so he could take an important call about the Telluride Festival, which he would be playing in.

"I'm looking at my face on your screen there," Peter said when we got the tape going again. The sun had shifted so our bench was pleasantly shady. A plate-sized white hibiscus blossom on the bush behind us occasionally grazed Peter's cloud of hair.

"You're looking good," I said. "I'd like to hear your poetic interpretation on something I came across. I think it ties into what we were discussing about spirituality and music. I read that what the human ear can hear at the farthest distance is birdsong. You can surmise that where there is birdsong, there is maybe water, trees, and other animals. In other words, life."

"Interesting you say that," said Peter. "A friend of mine, Jack Loeffler, in Santa Fe, goes out into the canyons and records birdsong. He's cataloging this stuff for the University of New Mexico, I think. Also, do you know who Dr. Andrew Weil is?"

"The guy who has a television show?"

"Yes. He's another Richard Evans Schultes graduate. He's the go-to alternative medicine doctor and he's written many books. I was in Arizona, and I called Andrew. He told me to come over and play some songs. We had dinner. Some kind of wonderful homemade cactus stew. Andrew Weil and several people there. I started to sing. And they all started doing bird calls. I thought, *They've got to be kidding me.* But no, it was part of their ethos, the nature in the Southwest, which is vibrant. I'm singing one of my songs and they're going *tweet tweet choowee choowee*," he said, twirling his hands, like a bird flying around.

Mesmerized by his flying bird hand gesture, I continued.

"Where I was going with that," I said, "is that there's something about music that is older than language and it affects us on an emotional level like nothing else. Like you said, bluegrass can make you feel joy. I can cry listening to music. It affects parts of your brain that words can't convey."

"I think Orpheus, the Greek god, could communicate with music," said Peter. "The origin of music is birdsong. Interestingly during COVID, there was so little traffic, there were so many more birds. The birds were everywhere."

Peter took his hat off to scratch his head. His white feathery hair looked like delicate snow. Like snow from atop the Himalayas.

"When humans understand birds," I offered, "we will have reached another level of evolution."

"I'm sure you've heard of the Indigenous theories of birds," said Peter. "They are beings in between spiritual realms. I just read in *The New York Review of Books* about a book describing the patterns of migrating birds. They migrate thousands of miles. From Greenland and end up in the Yucatán. Only when the winds are right."

I talked about a book I'd read called *The Genius of Birds*, by Jennifer Ackerman, which explains the various intelligences of birds. That birds can memorize melodies up to four minutes long. That birds can navigate thousands of miles.

I continued, "We as human beings overlook the intelligence of nature. Of birds. And oceans. And when we can read the language of nature, there's some discovery in that. And that's, I think, where music comes from. Maybe the greatest answers in science can be found in the simplest of things. In the ruffling of leaves in the wind, for instance."

"That goes back to my early walks as a six-year-old," said Peter. "Getting the confidence to be alone out in the woods."

I asked Peter about his song "On the Blue Horizon." I mentioned that most of the references in the song, except for Patsy Cline, are to jazz musicians.

On the blue horizon, where all things are possible. Black and white people holding hands, with the great artists of our age leading the way. John Coltrane, Otis Redding, and Patsy Cline forging a new consciousness. A consciousness of social justice, of ecological awareness. Knowledge that we are interdependent, interconnected. Our bodies and minds bound up in a continuum, calling to mind the Haudenosaunee notion of Seven Generations. That we should consider how our actions impact people and circumstances seven generations hence. Seven generations and then into infinity. Wherever our evolution leads us perhaps we will become part of the loam of the forest floor, bound up with the trees, fungus, and moss. Into the gush and squash. Perhaps we will find ourselves flung across the universe; our evolved consciousness then able to negotiate intergalactic travel in the blink of an eye. But why stop there? Perhaps our evolved sentience will enable us to traverse interdimensional space. And who's to say that all these forms of travel aren't interrelated? As we begin to understand that language of the trees, the song of birds, we then receive the holy illuminations. Interesting that, in the Apache language, the root word for land is the same as the word for mind. Robin Wall Kimmerer, Potawatomi botanist, has written that planting is a form of listening. Plants communicate to us in slow and subtle ways. But we must listen to learn. After all, plants have been on the earth longer than all other beings. They've had time to figure things out. In some Native languages the term plant translates to "those who take care of us."[14]

Peter Rowan, Hermes Trismegistus, came to tear open the hermetically sealed secrets contained in the ancient tones. For buried in the ancient tones are the clues to salvation. To the Great Work. To our higher selves.

Getting back to my questions about "On the Blue Horizon," I asked, "What were you trying to say in that song?"

"That there's going to be a great rebirth of inspired music. You mentioned birdsong. Eric Dolphy said that he used to play to the birds. He used to practice bass clarinet. David Grisman and I got a hold of saxophone books, took up playing, answering the call of 'Free Jazz'! We weren't really learning the horn that well. But it was, 'Play whatever sounds you were making that were pushing a sonic boundary.' We did play out in the woods. In fact, we used to stand at each end of a meadow on my parents' farm and we'd start playing and walk towards each other. When we got to the center, we'd put the bells of our horns together and come up with tonal hybrid crazy sounds. But John Coltrane had just passed on and there were a lot of jazz musicians looking for a way to carry on. Bebop music had evolved to the spiritual music that Coltrane had developed. There was a band called the Far Cry up in Boston. Richard Martin played saxophone.

Richard Martin had started at the Harvard Divinity School and was working postgraduate with Richard Evans Schultes. Richard and I were studying the writings of Aristotle with Haven O'More."

"I like the unanswerable philosophy questions," I said. "The ones Native American and Eastern philosophies explore. Like, when does the day begin and are days sequential or just circular?"

"Deep questions," said Peter. "In the Spanish language there are many Arabic words. One of them is *madrugada*, which means just before the first light of dawn, or even a little bit before then. The deepest part of night. It's the time of highest inspiration. It's the time when most people are finally feeling the beginning of being awake. *Madrugada*."

"It's a time when people may have hypnagogic dreams," I said. "They're not quite dreaming. It's that time just before we dream."

"Yes, then there's the period called *la relumbre*, which means the afterglow of sunset, or the glow before dawn."

"Is that from Arabic, too?"

"That I'm not sure of. But there are different names for different parts of the night. *Madrugada* is sort of the bewitching hour maybe. The darkest hour before the dawn."

"When you walk the floors?"

"You're either inspired or you're unhinged. I hope I'm answering your questions," said Peter, looking at himself in the video recorder.

"You are. They're intended to be an open format." I paused, laughing a little, checking the time.

I wanted to talk to Peter about his *Dharma Blues* album. Stylistically, the song selections on the album are very eclectic. There are strong elements of American gospel and Indian traditional styles, yodels, chants, bluegrass, blues, country, and folk. Yet, I can imagine a gypsy band playing these songs. Peter is rarely a purist but mixes genres together and makes it all work. He also wrote all the songs. I cannot think of another album that so skillfully brings this unique blend of influences. The result is not forced or manufactured. Credit should be given to his band: Jody Stecher on banjo and Indian bass sitar, Nepalese musician Manose Singh on bamboo flutes, Hot Tuna/ Jefferson Airplane's Jack Casady on bass and bass balalaika. Gerald Patrick Korte played most of the trap drum. Casey Waits played drums on day-night sessions. His parts were included in the final mix. Gillian Welch, who contributes vocals on three songs. These terrific musicians help elevate Peter's vision.

Peter is not afraid of being provocative. He begins the song "Dharma Blues" singing, "Ain't no God up in heaven / Ain't no devil down below." And despite the "Dharma Blues" bluesiness, it's bound together with a trance-like rhythm. Even though you can dance to the songs, there is a philosophical complexity to the lyrics, describing Peter's exploration of Buddhist ideas of attachment. This notion is toyed with in the refrain "win when you lose," sung over and over. In "Vulture Peak," Peter quotes the "Heart Sutra": "Form is emptiness / Emptiness is form / On truth there's no deception / No I / No we / No nose / No tongue/ No taste / No conception."

"Why did you choose to do an album of Buddhist songs?" I asked, referring to *Dharma Blues*. "I wish you'd do more Buddhist influenced albums."

"That's what I was writing. I went to India in 1993. And I just found myself involved in the subject matter. I received some criticism for using the album name *Dharma Blues*. Someone had done an album in the sixties called *Dharma Blues*, Sandy Bull. But the way I feel is that everyone should do a *Dharma Blues* album. Ricky Skaggs should do a *Dharma Blues*. Let's hear what you really are about. I want to hear about what's your journey. Not just an album of old gospel tunes. The *Dharma Blues* is about *your* path. It's the blues because there's a longing and there's a loss. And finding the truth lies somewhere in between or beyond. A lot of those songs were written in India or Japan. But 'Wisdom Woman' was written in Texas. That song came directly from a dream, I just wrote it down. A woman spoke to me in my dream."

"What did she say again?"
"She said, 'You know, you know, you know, you know.'"

She's radiant as the bright sunrise
She's got the moonlight dancing in her eyes
She comes to me at the break of day
Chasing all my cares and blues away

We started to sing the song together. Peter nodded his head, then continued.

"Then she said, 'I'm the dance that made Hank Williams sing. I'm the song that made him dance.'"

I'd read somewhere that Peter credited Jerry Garcia, his late bandmate in *Old & In the Way* and the main creative force behind the Grateful Dead, as someone who would have understood his exotic explorations into the Tao of bluegrass. It was during this time that Peter became a student of Buddhism. He happened to see a poster one day for a class on Tara empowerment by Kalu Rinpoche, a Tibetan teacher, stapled onto a telephone pole outside the Doggie Diner on Van Ness in San Francisco. "One week we're playing rock and roll at Fort Mason, the next week the Karmapa is zapping us, a thousand people, with boundless compassion, at the same place!" said Peter when I asked him about studying with Kalu Rinpoche.

Perhaps it was no mistake that he saw that poster.

"On that same album, 'A River of Time' is really a gospel tune. I wrote the guitar riff in Jamaica. I was still contributing to the album over time. John Chelew, who was the producer, would take ideas that I brought to him and suggest, 'Why don't you make that into a song?' He put the guitar down on a track and made a loop, for instance. Then he said, 'Are there lyrics? Can you sing to this?' I'd say, 'I have this little poem called "The River of Time." Let me try that.' It became a real collaboration. The reason there is a sitar or harmonium sound is because Jody Stecher came in and played on a couple of tracks. He's a very erudite musician. He studied in India. The producer took those sections and added them to other songs and wove this, quote" — Peter made air quotes with his fingers — "'psychedelia' in there. But really it was just a couple of songs we used an Indian instrument on. I didn't produce the record. Although it was said, I think in *Rolling Stone*, that 'Rowan has chosen to,' I didn't choose anything. I just gave it to the producer. I liked what he was doing. I might have said to certain things, 'It's got to be more of this way.' It was wonderful to have a producer. I've only had a few producers. Jerry Douglas is one of my favorites. He'll get 'er done. He produced *Dustbowl Children*. I'd brought five songs to him, three of which we kept. Jerry said it's a take when you're not singing the lyrics. It's when the vocal starts to play with the time. It's a little counterpoint to the time, even. I didn't really know what my own solo performance was. What's a take? It's very hard to judge your own material. If there's one guy who really knows how I make music, it's Jerry Douglas. Now John Chelew is the other one. For years he was the booking guy at McCabe's Guitar Shop in Los Angeles. It was an acoustic showcase. The other producer I worked with was George Martin. And Peter Siegel, who produced Earth Opera. On the Earth Opera album, we were all on a learning curve to some degree. And learning to overdub. I remember being frustrated in the studio at times. The attachment to music, as an expression of something deep, being thwarted by technology can be very frustrating. I haven't done an overdub record in thirty years. But I see a way to highlight what I want to highlight about bluegrass using this technology. For one, if you overdub parts, you can present them to the user's ear in a way, that is, the overtones might be clearer not absorbed in the general fray of the sound. In bluegrass there's so much going on, there are so many notes. Bill Monroe didn't like that either. He referred to that as, 'Note, note, note just to be note.' Bill Monroe favored simplicity, elegance, being true to the melody, and pure harmony."

"You kept a relationship with Bill Monroe after you left his group?"

"Yes."

"What did he think about your direction in music?"

"*It ain't no part of bluegrass,*" said Peter, mimicking Monroe's accent. "In those years of the eighties when I was in Nashville, I made a point of seeing Bill. I even worked up enough nerve to ask for a share of royalties for 'Walls of Time.' He wouldn't budge, but then he would sort of budge. He'd say, 'I can't see you today, I got a horse that's got loose. Call me next Monday. No, don't call me Monday, there'll be too much on me.' The thing is Bill was caught up in his cycles of worldly commitments, but the business end of things got a little bit muddied. He was already in the business fifty years when I met him. He wasn't going to let a kid have a piece of a song that he started. I asked Vassar Clements about that. I said, 'Vassar, how do you feel when Bill would do an instrumental on something you played?' And Vassar said, 'Pete, to me, it was just an honor.' And that's how it was seen in those days. That it was an honor that the star would take your idea. Especially someone on Bill's musical level. When I went back to Nashville in the eighties it was all about co-writing. I was involved in a publishing deal with Ricky Skaggs' company. You were expected to sit down every day with writers and co-write, churn them out. The publishing companies felt that this was the most efficient way to come up with new songs. And so, once I'd understood that I'd co-wrote a song, in fact given it its title, 'Walls of Time,' yes it was an honor, but it caused problems. When Bill thinks he could just take from you your artistic input then he doesn't feel like he has to pay you for it. Or the gig you just did. In the end Bill wound up owing me money and left it to me to keep asking. That's not right, it creates carelessness.

"You can't take it with you. One thing that Eric Clapton and his manager Robert Stigwood did was they created a royalty stream for all his musicians. When I was working with Jamie Oldaker, we'd go to the bank and I'd hear 'Lay Down Sally' and I'd say, 'Cha-ching, Jamie.' Jamie would still be getting those dollars. That's what my manager has done for me, is allow me to provide income streams for my musicians. But that's not how Bill saw it. My friend, the poet Charles Barnes, reminded me that Bill Monroe was from an agriculture background. To him, you were a tenant farmer. He'll get most of the crops and you got what you needed to live."

"Bill Monroe had a tough life. He was protective of what he'd made. There were elements of bluegrass that existed before. Is it fair to say that he invented bluegrass?"

"He wanted a certain drive in the music that, until he got Earl Scruggs in the band playing banjo, wasn't there. Bluegrass already had this rolling forward gait, but it also had a ragtime feeling. He took the young Flatt and Scruggs to New Orleans. He said, 'They were green and I had to take them to some place where they could learn.' And I said, 'What did you hear in New Orleans?' And Bill said, 'You could find anything in New Orleans.' Then he said, 'You had the jump time, which is that four on the floor. Then there's sock time which is more on the two.' Jump time became what we think of as boogie-woogie. Then bebop. Then Bill said, 'Of course, you have the slow drag.' The slow drag is that low-down like 'Since my baby left me.' When I started to go to New Orleans there was a bass player named Slow Drag something. He just put that drag in there. Bluegrass tempo is made up of all these things. But because

Bill Monroe played ahead of the beat, people tend to forget the other elements."

"What did Earl Scruggs' rolling fingerstyle bring to the band?"

"When Earl Scruggs came along there was real magic. And Earl and Lester were quick to realize they had taken Bill Monroe's music to new heights. It took a long time for Bill to acknowledge that. In the end, there was a lot between them, but they made up. When he was about fifty-six, after I had left the band, Bill met Julia LaBella who lives in Texas now, wonderful lady. They broke up after some time, but she came back to Bill when he was in his eighties. Of course, Bill's family was a little bit alarmed. Was she gold-digging? But Julia was just there. She'd been there for so long in his history. I did an interview with her at Earl Fest. I asked Julia, 'What was the most interesting thing about Bill's life?' And she said, 'He wanted to make up with everyone. He no longer was a competitor.' Bill was the youngest of seven kids. And because he was the smallest, they lorded it over him. It made him incredibly determined. Gave him time to think about how he wanted to approach things. Julia said, 'We would make phone calls, and go around to see everybody.' Everybody that had been competitive with him or had been enemies with him. He made up with everybody. I never expected that answer. I saw him back in the eighties, I would say let's get together, have lunch. I remember him looking at me and laughing, saying, 'Pete, them were good days,' when we were talking about our times together. When you're in your twenties and you're working with someone like Bill Monroe who's in his fifties, they've got a big advantage over you. I remember when Richard Greene joined the band. Bill asked him to drive the bus. But Richard said that he didn't have a license. And that was it, end of story. Bill wasn't going to second guess him. Richard was smart. He curtailed that obligation, whereas I would have said, 'Of course I'll drive your bus.'

"The other thing that she said was that once a month he would stand in the middle of the barnyard and turn every motor in the barn. While the tractor, the limo, the pickup truck, and anything else that had a motor was on, Bill would stand in the middle. And I started roaring with laughter because I thought that was so Bill Monroe, listening to all the farm tools. Then she said, if he heard a motor skipping, he knew you could put a new spark plug in there and know that it wasn't going to break the next month. To hear all of that at once. Mowers, tractors, and trucks. And that's how he would stay on top of it."

"You couldn't listen to each motor one at a time? Sounds like bluegrass to me."

"I think that says something about Bill's sensibility."

"Did you ever feel like you wanted to play with one band for a long time?"

"I was sorry to leave every group I'd ever left. When I left Seatrain and they got a replacement, I thought the band had improved. It would have been interesting to have another role in that band, not being *the* rhythm guitarist. Al Cooper saw Seatrain and said, 'You could be the front man.' I said, 'I don't know.'

"Same thing when I left Bill Monroe."

I asked Peter, "What is the hardest thing about being a leader in the bluegrass world?"

Peter then quoted Bill Monroe, "'When they finally learn the music, they want to leave and go out on their own.' And after three years that was me and I felt very sad. But I don't know if the music could have improved anymore. To not record 'Walls of Time'—I thought, 'What am I doing here?' I was twenty-five. Our generation was coming of age. Bill had done a bunch of college concerts but mostly we were playing for people that were Bill's age, or who were in their sixties. I distinctly remember I could stay on after I decided to leave. Why? Because all the reasons you decided to leave don't matter anymore. But you're not allowed to."

As Peter spoke, a California scrub jay alighted on a wooden fence that surrounded the café's backyard. Considering everything we'd just talked about I was struck by this. And Peter was too. As I had read in *The Genius of Birds*, recent research has suggested that western scrub jays, along with several other corvids, are among the most intelligent of animals. Scrub jays are the only non-primate or non-dolphin shown to plan. And studies have indicated that scrub jays can remember locations of over 200 food caches. More than that, they can remember each food item in each cache and its rate of decay. Because scrub jays pilfer, they are very good at concealing information, or providing false information. Like researchers say, "It takes a thief to catch a thief." In other words, scrub jays consider the perspective of others. California scrub jays also summon others to screech over the body of a dead jay, according to research from the University of California, Davis. The birds' cacophonous "funerals" can last for up to half an hour. For a day or two thereafter, they avoid feeding in the area. They remember their dead. Interesting to note that the scrub jay is a corvid, the same family as a raven.

"Do you ever dream about Bill Monroe?" I asked, though I was supposed to have asked my last question. The truth is I didn't want this moment to end. I wanted it to stretch on indefinitely. I felt an abiding love for Peter at that moment. Maybe the scrub jay was that love materialized. The scrub jay seemed to be a sign of some kind. I don't know if it was an incarnation of Bill Monroe or the universe trying to talk to us.

"He's always on my mind."

"I love your imitations of Bill Monroe."

"Once Bill had me in the band, he had someone who wasn't afraid to ask questions. That's how I know about New Orleans and anecdotes about him. Bill once said to me, 'Pete, when the music's right you will feel like you're flying. And then you can hear the ancient tones.' It wasn't you hear the ancient tones and so you go and try to make them. You make the music and the ancient tones emerge. You follow the musical rules, but you're not invested in them. The ancient tones emerge from the application of selflessness. As I said that I'm thinking of African kora music, the fantastic 6/8 timing that runs through it. *One two three four five six seven eight, one two three four five six seven eight* and so on. In bluegrass that is there. That's the problem. Interpretation of timing, as Bill would call it, is thought of as *four against three, or one two three, one two three, within the context of 4/4 time,* but there's a rhythmic harmonic overtone that's happening. It's the earliest rhythm of human beings, which of course is like a gallop. *Dat dat dat dat dat dat.*"

"Like those hayrides he was trying to recreate in music."

I was reminded of a dream I'd had a few days before talking to Peter. I was at a summer home that was also some kind of portal. I could feel the presence of aliens and other beings behind the walls. When I left, someone put an adhesive acid tab on my face, and I started tripping. I ran into Peter, who was a train conductor. When I got on the train, I had to hold on, upside down, as we roared through the subway tunnel— but it was more like a roller coaster. I was laughing and crying, saying I wouldn't want to be anywhere else. Peter told me that I was making too much noise. The subway tunnel became a mall. People going into shops. The train stopped. My mobile phone was still in my hand. I slid it into my shorts pocket and zipped it. The train took off again.

"Bill told me to follow the horse's hooves. It's very important because if you listen to African music, they never let the square four or eight bar measures, or even number of measures dominate and early on Bill Monroe played that on the mandolin. Bill was playing 6/8 over 4/4 time which allowed for that forward roll that Earl Scruggs brought in. That was the meshing of the musical patterns. The forward roll on the banjo is made up of three fingers. That's a three. It's not four fingers. Over a 4/4. It's the *and*. *One two three four* and *a one two three four*. The backbeat. 'The Great American Eagle Tragedy' tried to explore that."

As bluegrass scholar Thomas Goldsmith wrote in *Earl Scruggs and the Foggy Mountain Breakdown*, when Scruggs was a boy, "Some folks in North Carolina, mostly farther west, still make banjos out of gourds and without frets, in the style of African instruments that came to the South from West Africa in the eighteenth century. Many players used some version of the style called down-picking, in which a player brushes the strings downward with fingernails of the right hand. The technique also calls for the thumb to hit a short drop string in a rhythmic contrast that can get quite complicated. That style, too, was an African holdover."

Then Peter started clapping the beat, as cars beeped their horns, as if trying to conspire in this musical revelation. I wasn't sure if I completely understood it. But I knew I was hearing something at the burning center of a billion galaxies. I was hearing Peter Rowan transmit an ancient wisdom that he'd acquired from his musical lineage. The music combined science, spirituality, thumping heartbeat rhythms, and esoteric math. It was the source of what it is to be human.

After clapping Peter added, "It's in the music. For a moment in time that all came together in bluegrass. And then bluegrass became *bluegrass*. But nobody picked it up from there."

The clapping called to mind the idea of being awake. Of being awake in every moment. Attention, like the first word of Aldous Huxley's *Island*.

"Does bluegrass have a future?"

"This is what I sit around and talk to Christopher Henry about. How do we get that back in bluegrass? How do we bring the alchemy back into the sound? The *one two three four AND a one two three four.* The inner beauty of bluegrass is in those kinds of things but not many people pick up on it. If you listen to Béla Fleck, he has it in his bones."

To my mind *one two three four* echoed the birdsong chant *tweet tweet choowee choowee.* Perhaps birdsong is the source of rhythm and melody for humans.

Peter looked down at my phone camera sitting in its cradle. I hoped I hadn't worn him out with our two-and-a-half-hour-long conversation. But it looked like I might have.

"Did you get that last part?" he asked.

"I got the whole thing," I said.

"Because that's the answer to the whole question."

"When you were talking, I was thinking about the Pythagorean theory," I said. "When you place these things down in the right way, an illumination happens. When you use the right technical forms, but with that added feeling. And that's how the ancient tones surface. *It's not the what of the what you think you think you're thinking, it's the when.*"

As we walked to our cars, Peter and I chatted a bit more, cracking jokes. I was already missing him. But I'd see him again, in my dreams and elsewhere. I knew it.

When it was time to say goodbye, I asked if I could give him a hug. He agreed and not reluctantly. I was electrified by the channel of energy that just flowed through me. By some completely random combination of events, I found myself sitting at a table with Peter Rowan discussing the nature of the universe, like I'd cupped a lightning bolt in my hands. A portal had opened in the cosmos.

It reminded me of a dream I'd had as a kid. In the dream I awoke and looked at my body, which was illuminated. It occurred to me suddenly that I was alive and conscious. That I was me. And that being me is like being you.

As Anthony Peake wrote in his essay *What is the best available evidence for the survival of human consciousness after permanent bodily death?*: "I have been informed by Danny Rubin, the original script writer of *Groundhog Day*, that he imagined Connors repeating the day 3,652,500 days (10,000 years). According to Buddhist beliefs on reincarnation, after that specific number of 'turns of the potter's wheel' (Dukkha), the soul can progress to Nirvana or, in Connors' case, February 3rd."

The Vortex

One day when Rama was playing with the other sons of the cowherds, his mother, Yasoda, received a report from the other boys.

"Rama has eaten dirt," they told her.

Yasoda slapped Rama's hand, scolded him, and said, "Naughty boy, why have you secretly eaten dirt?"

Rama replied, "Mother, I have not eaten dirt. They are lying. If you think they speak the truth, look at my mouth yourself."

"Open your mouth so I can see," she demanded.

Rama opened his mouth.

Peering in his mouth, Yasoda saw trees of every kind, loams of mycorrhizal fungi that web across the earth, blue and red oceans on different planets; she saw the wind, and lightning, and the moon and stars, Jupiter and Mars, and the zodiac; and the space beyond space. She saw how one can master their senses as well as how sentient beings can be conquered and destroyed by their senses. In Rama's gaping mouth, Yasoda saw the multiverse, beings from different realms; she saw all times and places; she beheld all nature and action and hopes. Suddenly she remembered her own little village and her world. Then she felt small and claustrophobic. Confused and frightened, her mind began racing.

Is my world small and stupid? Am I a fool? Am I imagining all this? Is this sorcery? Or is my son a god? If he is a god, I will bow down at his feet.

Yasoda sat down and began to breathe. Slowly.

Many days passed.

Then decades.

Then eons passed.

A million universes passed into oblivion.

A billion billion universes were born.

Still sitting, tears rolling down her face, Yasoda thought to herself.

I now understand that I cannot fathom what I have seen.

But she wasn't afraid any longer.

I can be tricked by false beliefs such as "I" and "you." I realize that all sentience is connected. And not just sentience. All universes are connected, interwoven and a part of each other.

When Yasoda had come to this understanding, she lost the memory of what had previously occurred. She took Rama in her arms, hugging and kissing him, saying, "I love you so much my sweet little boy."

My Love Will Never Change[15]

During his journeys, Padmasambhava met Yeshe Tsogyal, who became his consort and then his archivist.[16] It was said that Tsogyal was often seen silently mouthing Tibetan prayers while holding prayer beads close to her heart. Yeshe Tsogyal's hair was adorned with a dangling blue coral pendant.

Like Padmasambhava, she was an immensely powerful mystic. Yeshe Tsogyal memorized and privately recited Padmasambhava's teachings and instructions, keeping them hidden from those who would corrupt them. The teachings were only transmitted or whispered from lips to lips. Yeshe Tsogyal learned that the key to understanding Padmasambhava's wisdom was embracing its emphasis on compassion. Even the great sages could be too focused on their own mastery of meditation and prayer. But prayer and meditation were merely techniques. The true essence of Padmasambhava's teachings lie in controlling one's own sense of self-aggrandizement. If not grounded in love and humility, Padmasambhava's teachings could even be dangerous. Being enamored of one's own wisdom, while forsaking the benefit of others, had ruined many great magicians. They had become obsessed with their own reflection. A dangerous dead end.

Having arrived in the Land of the Dakinis, Yeshe Tsogyal had a vivid vision of radiant light. In this land, instead of leaves, spikes hung from the trees. The ground was plastered with flesh. The mountains were bristling piles of skeletons and the clods of earth and stone were scattered fragments of bone. In the center of this abomination was an immeasurable palace built of skulls and severed heads. The building was ringed by a circle of volcanoes, a wall of *vajras*, a perimeter of falling thunderbolts, a ring of eight cemeteries and a wall of beautiful lotuses. Within this boundary were flocks of flesh-eating, blood-drinking ravens and crowds of demon savages.

Suddenly, Yeshe Tsogyal found herself surrounded by fiends, red blood dripping from their open mouths, glaring at her threateningly. There were ghosts swirling around the charnel ground whispering, "give us a drink of wine" and "give us a bite of bread."[17]

Her hands clasped in prayer, Yeshe Tsogyal now sang out at the top of her lungs.

"My love will never change," she proclaimed, her voice like clapping thunder. Suddenly a great wind swept over the land, quaking the ground, and toppling the mountains of skeletons in its wake. Her voice roared like a thousand chainsaws, lawnmowers, trucks, and the groan of a million dying stars. It echoed throughout a billion universes.

But it was also a cry of love.

Yeshe Tsogyal then rushed towards the demons. As they backed away from her, she began dancing. She danced the dance of the love of ages and the love of all things. And as she danced, Yeshe Tsogyal began to chant and sing, "Let every living breathing being find happiness."[18]

Even the demons were now spellbound by Yeshe Tsogyal. She had opened their hearts with her boundless love and compassion. With her arms wide open, she embraced the demons, holding them lovingly to her chest. She even let them drink her blood, but only to nourish themselves. They swarmed around her, drawn by her affection, and made gentle by her compassion.

In another vision, Yeshe Tsogyal beheld a manifestation of Padmasambhava called the Immense Vajra Ocean. In this vision, each pore in Padmasambhava's body held one billion realms and, in each realm, there were one billion universes. In each of these universes there were one billion Padmasambhavas, who each created one billion emanations. Each of these emanations was responsible for training one billion disciples.

For a thousand years, Yeshe Tsogyal taught innumerable disciples how to discern the true nature of being. To see all phenomena as dreams, castles in the air, reflections of the midnight moonlight. When she was ready, she ascended bodily into the Paradise of the Dakinis, a retinue of disciples accompanying her, singing in unison.

Because of Yeshe Tsogyal's writings, Padmasambhava's lineage was carried down, across the rolling hills,[19] from saint to saint, from holy person to holy person, murmured from lips to lips, through the ages. You could say that because of Yeshe Tsogyal's writings, I met Peter Rowan again in this particular incarnation of the universe.

Harry Smith, American Magus

In 1996, I went to see *Harry Smith, American Magus*, a documentary directed by Paola Igliori, at Anthology Film Archives in the East Village. Harry Smith was a visual artist, filmmaker, mystic, alchemist, record collector, student of anthropology, and an important figure in the New York beat scene. Among his many achievements, Smith compiled the *Anthology of American Folk Music* in 1953. The anthology brought together blues, ballads, social music, religious and spiritual songs, bluegrass, and more. At that time, American music was segregated by race more overtly than it is today. Smith compiled the songs in such a way that listeners of the anthology didn't always know the identity of the musicians. People just heard the songs. The music of the Carter Family, Blind Willie Johnson, Mississippi John Hurt, and others had significant influence on generations of songwriters and musicians like Peter Rowan, Bob Dylan, the Beatles—really the list is too long to include here. Smith's anthology is still influencing songwriters today.

The *Anthology of American Folk Music* isn't specifically a bluegrass collection. But there is no doubt that the musicians included helped shape bluegrass—for instance, Maybelle Carter's guitar playing is one of the cornerstones of guitar picking that deeply influenced bluegrass artists like Clarence White, Norman Blake, and Peter Rowan. Thomas Goldsmith has noted that Lester Flatt's guitar playing employed an "old fashioned approach with a thumb pick and one fingerpick" that was reminiscent of Maybelle Carter's style.

Harry Smith, American Magus has priceless clips and interviews. One of my favorites is John Cohen talking to Harry Smith about Smith's meeting with Sara Carter of the Carter Family. He went to visit Sara to examine the quilts that she had sown by hand. Always interested in how one art corresponds to another, Harry was exploring how Sara's quilts related to her music. During the interview John asked Smith about his extensive peyote experiences.

"Where did you first take peyote?" Cohen asked.

Smith said, "On the road to Sara Carter's."

I had watched the documentary many times over a period of twenty-five years, and after the 1996 screening, I reached out to Paola Igliori and got a copy of the film. A few years ago, I wrote again and asked Paola if she'd mind my digitizing it. She was delighted and called me on FaceTime immediately from Italy, reporting that the original copies were not in great shape. After I shared the digitized copy with her, Paola said that it might be the only existing viewable copy of the documentary.

I sent Peter a link to the documentary, thinking that he'd want to see the film. He wrote back saying, "I have to tell you my Harry Smith story."

Positively 4th Street

I couldn't wait to speak with Rowan again and we connected next in July 2021. He told me about meeting Harry Smith in Greenwich Village.

"We had driven up from Nashville along old Highway 17 through all the little towns along the way; up through the Shenandoah Valley of Virginia and finally through the Holland Tunnel into the Big Apple. Bill Monroe and the Bluegrass Boys had come north to play the Newport Folk Festival. We had driven straight through, about twenty hours, in the old bus, the Bluegrass Special. We parked on West 4th Street in Greenwich Village. I had been driving so I took a late afternoon nap at Ralph Rinzler's apartment, in a hand-built chestnut wood bed, under beautiful quilts from the Southern Mountains. Ralph was a collector of handmade Southern mountain crafts and was booking acts at the Newport Folk Festival. I was exhausted, sleeping soundly, when about five in the evening I slowly began to awaken to the sounds of conversations, chattering in various accents, dialects, deep Southern accents, Irish brogue, French Canadian accents, like the whole ethnic world of folk music had arrived and were speaking all at once in Ralph's apartment. As I was under the comfy handmade quilts right there in the living room and there was no escape. People were gathering and chatting and took no notice of me, as if it were perfectly normal for a sleeping Bluegrass Boy to be there half-awake in a chestnut wood bed under colorful quilts in the middle of a party! I began to chuckle quietly at the surreal quality of the situation. Then I began to lose it. All the various accented voices now roosting like a wayward flock of ravens in my head! Ralph saw me slipping into hysterical laughter, and the kind mentor that he was, he guided me giggling to the door and upstairs to another apartment where a thin, elvish, wispy-bearded man greeted us. It was the wizard, Harry Smith. Harry Smith then proceeded to entertain me for several hours with his movies, his photographic slides of designs of fabrics and weaving from cultures around the world. He showed my whirling mind the Seminole patterns of sown fabrics, and their reverse images from the inside, Scottish tartans and their mystical patterns, Kiowa Apache dance regalia from Anadarko, Oklahoma. He played me films he had created, hand drawn frame by frame; he was tireless, showing me that patterns and voice, musical sounds, were all interrelated, were reflections of the inside, the outside, and all in-between. I would be guided to Anadarko, Oklahoma on a future vision quest.

"Harry Smith would later spend his later days in residence at Naropa University in Boulder, Colorado, brought there by Allen Ginsburg. Naropa, named after an enlightened Buddhist master, was the creation of Chögyam Trungpa, the Eleventh Trungpa Tulku of the Marpa Ear-Whispered lineage, descended from the enlightened Buddhist master, poet-singer Milarepa. Every time I had the good fortune to play in the Boulder, Colorado area, Harry Smith would be in the front row, his bright eyes attentive to every sound, every nuance. He heard the deeper patterns and saw the great mandala. For a disciple to sing for the master is the highest honor!

"When I played festivals in Boulder during the 1980s all my good friends from Hot Rize were out there. Peter Wernick, Nick Forster, Tim O'Brien, and Charles Sawtelle. Charles Sawtelle was a very dear friend, and I would often visit with him. And I would ask Charles, 'How are we going to bridge this gap between this hidebound bluegrass thing with modern expression?' And guess what Charles played me?"

I had no idea.

"Charles played me Yungchen's first record and said, 'Look what she's done.' And I said, 'Right.' I'd already written 'Land of the Navajo' at this point. But where do you go with the free jazz influence and the hardcore formal arrangements? I never knew what I wanted to do. Only now has it finally clarified with my band the Free Mexican Airforce. At the time I heard Yungchen's record I didn't know whether to sing mantras or keep going in bluegrass."

And to think I know Peter Rowan from meeting Yungchen. Originally from a remote village in Tibet, Yungchen fled her home country, her son strapped to her back, and found her way to Australia, where she achieved international acclaim. It was no mistake that we all had connected; we'd known each other in previous cycles of life.

"Who Will Live" (Peter Rowan, *Dharma Blues*)
Time, illusion
Time grows weary, growing old
Lost in confusion
Reaching out someone to hold

What do you really want?
What do you really want?

Who will live, will love, will laugh, will cry
Who will live, will love, will never die
Who will sing, will dance, who will laugh, who will cry
Who will live, will love, will never die

That's what you really want
That's what we really want

What we really want

I Have Been Illusion's Fool[20]

I had a dream weeks after our meeting. In the dream, I was given a sacred object, perhaps by extraterrestrials. The object looked benign. When I looked closer, I saw a likeness of a green and purple Yoda Buddha. But the image could only be discovered by holding the object sideways and upside down. Like the way you might suddenly "hear" the encoded messages in bluegrass. You had to discover the primer to truly "hear" it. You had to come to this realization.

It was as if a hysterical cosmic joke had been revealed to me, telling me that the mind is formed of constructs that are built on yet more atomic constructs and that this miniaturization continues into emptiness. Yes, we have agency, but we are enmeshed in history. Our minds are trapped in the context in which they are formed. Dreams, meditations, psychedelic experiences may help us see through the illusion, but even those epiphanies are ephemeral. We are star stuff. Dust accumulated. The wind can blow us away. And while logic is vital to our existence, compassion is our compass.

Peter Rowan, like all of us, has lived many lives. In this incarnation, he is Hermes Trismegistus, Padmasambhava, cowboy Buddha, jokester, singer, Bluegrass Boy, father, brother, and mentor.

Mining the magical forms of bluegrass, Peter transformed its ancient tones into the language of a new generation. The ancient tones take us to a place of transcendence or paradise. Paradise comes from the Persian *pairidaeza*, meaning "park" or "enclosed garden." It suggests an intermediate state between incarnation and bliss. The enclosed garden is a primal state, charged with vitality and possibility.

Peter wasn't content to only play traditional bluegrass. Others tried to copy Bill Monroe, but Peter Rowan transmuted the music of Monroe and his predecessors into something new.

"Panama Red" isn't just another cowboy song. It is the product of Peter's alchemy. "Panama Red" contains the history of the cosmos. It possesses powers that charge you to dance and sing. That make you want to kiss and embrace one another. Its rapture inspires you to a holy state. A state of pure love and joy.

Having stewed a billion years in the snowy Himalayas, "Panama Red" was dipped in psychedelia, then passed through the vortex of Harry Smith's *Anthology of American Folk Music* only to be shrouded in the sounds of Bill Monroe's bluegrass. The Panama Red of the song is the reincarnated Padmasambhava that comes riding on his white horse to bring magic to the suffering people of the West.

> "Across the Rolling Hills (Padmasambhava)" (Peter Rowan, *Legacy*)
> On My Wind Horse at sunrise, I come riding.
> On My Wind Horse at sunrise, we're dancing in the sky.
> Padmasambhava comes riding.
> Om Ah Hung Vajra Guru Padma Siddhi Hung.

The Gourd Really Tied Everything Together

This story begins at the end. It is the dream that dreams the dreamer.

It was in Juan Carlos Pinto's studio that I discovered Ernie Paniccioli's portrait. This set off a chain of events that are bound together by a magical gourd.

Originally from Guatemala, residing now in Brooklyn, Pinto is stout and handsome. Like the carving on the sarcophagus of the Mayan spaceman, K'inich Janaab Pakal I, also known as Pacal, Pinto has a hooked nose, heavy eyelids, and curled lips. Pinto is the kind of artist who is always at work. He has busy hands. He paints, creates mosaics using found objects and discarded porcelain, tiles, et cetera, and works in other mediums as well. Pinto has distinguished himself by making portraits of famous artists and public figures from bits of New York City MTA cards.

If we're outside on the roof of his studio, Pinto is working on a project. When we're sitting in his studio, crowded with paintings, statues, and other objects, some completed, some in progress, Pinto is working. We've moved inside and outside the same night due to rain, or to escape the freezing cold, and Pinto begins working on whatever is in front of him.

Pinto is a hub. He brings artists together. They are a very inspiring group of people. We even drink and party. I affectionately call him Pintolino.

One night, it was just the two of us at the studio, I pointed to a portrait that was hiding behind others.

"Who is that?" I asked.

"That's Brother Ernie," said Pinto. Brother Ernie is how many people refer to Paniccioli. A legendary hip-hop photographer, Ernie was born in Brooklyn, of Cree and

Italian-American parents, and grew up in a tough section of Bedford-Stuyvesant. He was teased for being of Indigenous origin. Overcoming these challenges bestowed on Ernie a unique perspective, made him strong willed and bold. Many hip-hop artists are also from places like Bedford-Stuyvesant. And their talent made them different. Because of their similar experiences, they trusted Ernie. Ernie's understanding of their world is reflected in the way he captured these artists in pictures. We don't just see their fancy clothes and diamond rings. We see their souls.

I've seen many portraits in Pinto's studio. But his rendering of Brother Ernie really spoke to me. There was a hint of a smile, but the face wasn't smiling. The eyes appeared full of tears, but they weren't crying. Pinto managed to express a living essence behind the eyes in this portrait.

"You want to meet him?"

"Definitely," I said. I had been writing a series of interviews with Indigenous Americans, trying to convey personal histories in the context of the larger historical picture.

"I'll introduce you."

Sometime later, I introduced myself to Ernie in a Facebook message.

"I'm a friend of Pinto's," I said. "Check out this article I wrote."

I sent Ernie a story that I had written about Roman Perez, a Brooklyn-based Taíno chief.

"You were very respectful and gentle in what you wrote," replied Ernie. "I'll do an interview with you."

I then wrote an article about his Cree background, growing up in Brooklyn, and career as a hip-hop photographer. A few months later, I drove with Pinto to New Jersey to hand-deliver the portrait to Brother Ernie. It was a very moving experience.

Afterwards Ernie introduced me to Yungchen Lhamo. I never asked him to make an introduction.

"Do you want to interview a world-famous Tibetan singer?" he wrote in a Facebook message.

"Yes," I replied.

"Take care of her; she's very special," said Ernie.

While writing this book, I stumbled upon and began reading *Buddha in Redface*, a novel by Eduardo Duran. It's a fabulous story that reads like an autobiography. Duran is a psychologist of Indigenous origins serving his community in New Mexico, helping people who suffer from trauma, depression, and alcoholism. During his outreach, he met Tarrence, an older man who, due to illness, was completely restricted to his bed. Eduardo quickly realized that Tarrence was a particularly wise human being. Without going too much into the details, a gourd that is central to the story reverses bad deeds that Eduardo's ancestor committed.

Then one day I was on Pinto's roof. He disappeared into his studio, leaving me alone. The sky was chalky white. The sun was setting, but it was hidden behind clouds. As I sat on a folding chair, drinking a beer, Pinto returned to the roof with a white gourd in his hand. He picked petals and leaves from various flowerpots and placed them in the gourd.

This was magical, but I kept that thought to myself. Pinto would probably laugh at me if I spoke it aloud. I'd never seen the gourd in his studio before. As Pinto moved around the roof with the gourd, I was witnessing a ritual.

"I love the smell," said Pinto, whiffing the area around the gourd.

Many cultures, of course, use gourds to carry and pour water. Gourds also appear in many creation myths. According to Taíno mythology, all the world's waters were issued from a gourd. The story explains that Yaya, the elemental being of creation and life-giver, decided to expel his son Yayael for attempting to kill him. Yaya finally kills his son, storing his bones in a gourd. In time, Yayael's bones metamorphosed into fish. After a while, mother earth, Itiba Cahubaba, who was created by Yaya, died giving birth to four children. Deminán Caracaracol, one of the four, picked up the gourd, mistakenly dropping it. As the gourd smashed on the floor, it broke, gushing out water, creating all the oceans, rivers, and seas.

Gourds have been used for food, kitchen tools, toys, and decorations. Maracas and sitars are made from gourds. The guiro, a Latin American percussion instrument, is made from a gourd, as are many African percussion instruments.

The African kora, a string instrument previously mentioned in this book, is also made from a gourd. During one of our conversations, Peter said that bluegrass and African kora music share a continuous rolling rhythm technique. "It's the earliest rhythm of human beings," he explained. As if the rhythm of the gourd is what ties everything together.

I looked at the time on my phone. I was waiting for a text from Peter. We had to talk that day. But I wanted to be home to take the call.

I stayed longer on Pinto's roof than I had intended that day. Then I received the text from Peter. Just as I was about to leave, a heavy rain began to pour from the sky. I walked briskly home on Coney Island Avenue, skipping over puddles, as buckets of water flooded the streets.

I called Peter to discuss the *Mescalito Riding His White Horse* manuscript. We had since moved beyond interviews into conversation—discussing literature, philosophy, esotericism, and life. Like I do with my best friends. Sharing knowledge, making jokes.

Peter recited and sang lyrics from a song he was working on. The song is about Jonah and his gourd. The Bible says, "And the Lord God prepared a gourd, and made it to come up over Jonah, that it might be a shadow over his head, to deliver him from his grief." The gourd is a source of joy for Jonah.

When Peter began reading his song lyrics to me, I briefly went into a dream state. Into the dreamtime. Like a bell had tolled in my head. I loved Peter's poem, but, in my mind, I kept seeing Pinto's likeness glide past me with the gourd in his hand. Sometimes he placed it on his head, wearing it like a top hat. Like a Grateful Dead skeleton. I chuckled. Then the gourd ballooned. Now Pinto was climbing a giant version of the gourd. It was shaped like a mushroom, red with white dots. Then he floated above the gourd, as if levitating. He looked like a Buddha. He put his index finger up to his lips, to hush me.

"Listen. Breathe," he said. "Be still."

As he smiled scrub jays gently landed on him, one on each shoulder.

I resumed the conversation with Peter. I was fully engaged, happy to be talking to him. I hoped our conversation would never end. After I hung up the phone, I sat on my couch rubbing my eyes. The living room in my apartment came back into focus. I put on "Walls of Time" and began daydreaming.

I had developed such a fondness, even a love, for Peter, that I hoped my conversations with him would go on forever. But of course, they will. As long as I follow the horse's hooves, I'll hear Peter murmuring his songs and prayers to me. Lifetime after lifetime.[21]

Endnotes

1. *Mescalito riding his white horse*, "Free Mexican Airforce" (Peter Rowan, *Peter Rowan*).
2. *I Have Sung Illusion's Songs*, "Illusion's Fool" (Peter Rowan, *Dharma Blues*).
3. *Mescalito riding his white horse*, "Free Mexican Airforce" (Peter Rowan, *Peter Rowan*).
4. *Sailing on the river of time*, "River of Time" (Peter Rowan, *Dharma Blues*).
5. Peter Rowan - Free Mexican Air-Force - Whispering Beard Folk Festival 8/29/09 (https://www.youtube.com/watch?v=4dlFMKmE7pg).
6. Tsogyal, Yeshe, *The Lotus-Born: The Life Story of Padmasambhava*.
7. *Midnight Moonlight*, "Midnight Moonlight" (Peter Rowan, *Peter Rowan*).
8. *I have been illusion's fool*, "Illusion's Fool" (Peter Rowan, *Dharma Blues*).
9. Duran, Eduardo, *Buddha in Redface*.
10. Spira, Rupert, *Being Myself*.
11. *Freedom for us is a prison for the rulers of might*, "Free Mexican Airforce" (Peter Rowan, *Peter Rowan*).
12. *Who will live will love*, "Who Will Live" (Peter Rowan, *Dharma Blues*).
13. *Jewel of priceless worth*, "Restless Grave" (Peter Rowan, *Dharma Blues*).
14. Kimmerer, Robin Wall, *Braiding Sweetgrass*.
15. *My love will never change*, "My Love Will Never Change" (Peter Rowan, *Dharma Blues*).
16. Tsogyal, Yeshe, *Sky Dancer: The Secret Life and Songs of Yeshe Tsogyal*.

17. *Give us a drink of wine* and *give us a bite of bread*, "Restless Grave" (Peter Rowan, *Dharma Blues*).

18. *Let every living breathing being find happiness*, "Arise" (Peter Rowan, *Dharma Blues*).

19. *Across the Rolling Hills*, "Across the Rolling Hills (Padmasambhava)" (Peter Rowan, *Dharma Blues*).

20. *I have been illusion's fool*, "Illusion's Fool" (Peter Rowan, *Dharma Blues*).

21. *Lifetime after lifetime*, "Arise" (Peter Rowan, *Dharma Blues*).

Bibliography

These are sources either used or referenced while writing this book.

Books

Ackerman, Jennifer. *The Genius of Birds*. New York City: Penguin Books, 2017.

Beer, Robert. *Buddhist Masters of Enchantment*. Translated by Keith Dowman. Rochester, Vermont: Inner Traditions, 1988.

Duran, Eduardo. *Buddha in Redface*. Lincoln: Writers Club Press, 2000.

Goldsmith, Thomas. *The Bluegrass Reader*. Edited by Thomas Goldsmith. Champaign: University of Illinois Press, 2004.

Goldsmith, Thomas. *Earl Scruggs and the Foggy Mountain Breakdown*. Champaign: University of Illinois Press, 2019.

Huxley, Aldous. *Island*. New York: Harper & Brothers, 1962.

Huxley, Aldous. *Moksha*. Edited by Michael Horowitz and Cynthia Palmer. Rochester, Vermont: Park Street Press, 1977.

Huxley, Aldous. *The Perennial Philosophy*. New York: Harper & Brothers, 1945.

Kimmerer, Robin Wall. *Braiding Sweetgrass*. Canada; Minneapolis: Milkweed Editions, 2013.

Marcus, Greil. *Invisible Republic*. New York: Picador, 1997.

Matthews, Caitlín and John Matthews. *Walkers Between the Worlds: The Western Mysteries from Shaman to Magus*. Rochester, Vermont: Inner Traditions, 1985.

Peake, Anthony. *The Hidden Universe*. London: Watkins Publishing, 2019.

Peake, Anthony. *Opening the Doors of Perception*. London: Watkins Publishing, 2016.

The Ramayana. Translated by R. K. Narayan. London: Penguin Classics, 1972.

Rosenberg, Neil. *Bluegrass Generation*. Champaign: University of Illinois Press, 2018.

Spira, Rupert. *Being Myself*. Oakland: Sahaja Publications, 2021.

Tsogyal, Yeshe. *Dakini Teachings: A Collection of Padmasambhava's Advice to the Dakini*. Kathmandu: Rangjung Yeshe Publications, 1990.

Tsogyal, Yeshe. *The Lotus-Born: The Life Story of Padmasambhava*. Kathmandu: Rangjung Yeshe Publications, 1993.

Tsogyal, Yeshe. *Sky Dancer: The Secret Life and Songs of Yeshe Tsogyal*. Translated and commentary by Keith Dowman. Ithaca: Snow Lion Publications, 1996.

The Upanishads. Translated by Juan Mascaro. New York: Penguin Classics, 1965.

Wasson, R. Gordon. *The Wonderous Mushroom: Mycolatry in Mesoamerica*. San Francisco: City Lights Publishers, 2015.

Articles

Fiorito, Michael. "Peter Rowan's Musical Adventures." *Atwood Magazine*, 2021.

Fiorito, Michael. "Tibetan Artist Yungchen Lhamo Sings for a Better World." *Atwood Magazine*, 2021.

Miller, Tim. "Young Krishna & the Universe in His Mouth." *Word and Silence*, 2016.

Norbu, Konchog. "Bluegrass Buddhist Peter Rowan's Tibetan Collaboration, New Film." *Lion's Roar*, October 1, 2013.

Rowan, Peter. "Peter Rowan Bluegrass Band: The Fresh Air Interview." Interview by Terry Gross. *Fresh Air*, NPR, October 29, 2012, https://www.npr.org/transcripts/163874923.

Discography

Old & In the Way, Old & In the Way, Rounder (1975)

Peter Rowan, Flying Fish (1978)

Texican Badman, Appaloosa (1980)

The Walls of Time, Sugar Hill (1982)

All on a Rising Day, Sugar Hill (1991)
Legacy, Peter Rowan Bluegrass Band, Compass Records (2010)
Dharma Blues, Omnivore Recordings (2014)

Video Documentary

Igliori, Paola, dir. *Harry Smith, American Magus*. New York: Inanout Digital Productions, 2001. https://www.youtube.com/watch?v=s2XqGTn_8Xs&t=74s.

O-BOOKS

SPIRITUALITY

O is a symbol of the world, of oneness and unity; this eye represents knowledge and insight. We publish titles on general spirituality and living a spiritual life. We aim to inform and help you on your own journey in this life.

If you have enjoyed this book, why not tell other readers by posting a review on your preferred book site?

The Holy Spirit's Interpretation of the New Testament
A Course in Understanding and Acceptance
Regina Dawn Akers
Following on from the strength of *A Course In Miracles*, NTI
teaches us how to experience the love and oneness of God.
Paperback: 978-1-84694-085-9 ebook: 978-1-78099-083-5

The Message of A Course In Miracles
A translation of the Text in plain language
Elizabeth A. Cronkhite
A translation of *A Course in Miracles* into plain, everyday
language for anyone seeking inner peace. The companion
volume, *Practicing A Course In Miracles*, offers practical lessons
and mentoring.
Paperback: 978-1-84694-319-5 ebook: 978-1-84694-642-4

Your Simple Path
Find Happiness in every step
Ian Tucker
A guide to helping us reconnect with what is really important
in our lives.
Paperback: 978-1-78279-349-6 ebook: 978-1-78279-348-9

365 Days of Wisdom
Daily Messages To Inspire You Through The Year
Dadi Janki
Daily messages which cool the mind, warm the heart and
guide you along your journey.
Paperback: 978-1-84694-863-3 ebook: 978-1-84694-864-0

Body of Wisdom
Women's Spiritual Power and How it Serves
Hilary Hart
Bringing together the dreams and experiences of women across
the world with today's most visionary spiritual teachers.
Paperback: 978-1-78099-696-7 ebook: 978-1-78099-695-0

Dying to Be Free
From Enforced Secrecy to Near Death to True Transformation
Hannah Robinson
After an unexpected accident and near-death experience,
Hannah Robinson found herself radically transforming her
life, while a remarkable new insight altered her relationship
with her father, a practising Catholic priest.
Paperback: 978-1-78535-254-6 ebook: 978-1-78535-255-3

The Ecology of the Soul
A Manual of Peace, Power and Personal Growth for Real
People in the Real World
Aidan Walker
Balance your own inner Ecology of the Soul to regain your
natural state of peace, power and wellbeing.
Paperback: 978-1-78279-850-7 ebook: 978-1-78279-849-1

Not I, Not other than I
The Life and Teachings of Russel Williams
Steve Taylor, Russel Williams
The miraculous life and inspiring teachings of one of the
World's greatest living Sages.
Paperback: 978-1-78279-729-6 ebook: 978-1-78279-728-9

On the Other Side of Love
A woman's unconventional journey towards wisdom
Muriel Maufroy
When life has lost all meaning, what do you do?
Paperback: 978-1-78535-281-2 ebook: 978-1-78535-282-9

Practicing A Course In Miracles
A translation of the Workbook in plain language,
with mentor's notes
Elizabeth A. Cronkhite
The practical second and third volumes of The Plain-Language
A Course In Miracles.
Paperback: 978-1-84694-403-1 ebook: 978-1-78099-072-9

Quantum Bliss
The Quantum Mechanics of Happiness, Abundance, and
Health
George S. Mentz
Quantum Bliss is the breakthrough summary of success and
spirituality secrets that customers have been waiting for.
Paperback: 978-1-78535-203-4 ebook: 978-1-78535-204-1

The Upside Down Mountain
Mags MacKean
A must-read for anyone weary of chasing success and
happiness – one woman's inspirational journey swapping the
uphill slog for the downhill slope.
Paperback: 978-1-78535-171-6 ebook: 978-1-78535-172-3

Your Personal Tuning Fork
The Endocrine System
Deborah Bates
Discover your body's health secret, the endocrine system, and
'twang' your way to sustainable health!
Paperback: 978-1-84694-503-8 ebook: 978-1-78099-697-4

Readers of ebooks can buy or view any of these bestsellers by
clicking on the live link in the title. Most titles are published
in paperback and as an ebook. Paperbacks are available in
traditional bookshops. Both print and ebook formats are
available online.

Find more titles and sign up to our readers' newsletter at
http://www.johnhuntpublishing.com/mind-body-spirit Follow
us on Facebook at https://www.facebook.com/OBooks/ and
Twitter at https://twitter.com/obooks